THE
ESSENTIAL FLEET STREET

Its History and Influence

Ray Boston

BLANDFORD

Blandford
An imprint of Cassell
Villiers House, 41/47 Strand, London WC2N 5JE

First published 1990

Distributed in the United States by
Sterling Publishing Co., Inc.,
387 Park Avenue South, New York, NY 10016-8810

Distributed in Australia by
Capricorn Link (Australia) Pty Ltd,
PO Box 665, Lane Cove, NSW 2066

British Library Cataloguing in Publication Data
Boston, Ray, *1927–*
    The essential Fleet Street: its history and influence.
    1. London: (City). Fleet Street, history
    I. Title
    942.12

ISBN 0-7137-2136-7

Typeset by August Filmsetting, Haydock, St Helens

Printed and bound in Great Britain by Bath Press, Avon

THE ESSENTIAL FLEET STREET

Contents

To my wife, Elizabeth

Acknowledgements

Over many years of wide-ranging reading and personal investigations, I have incurred many debts of gratitude. For particular kindnesses I wish to thank the following: David Linton for handling the pictures and the index; A. J. P. Taylor for putting me right on the subject of 'The Troublemakers'; Louis Heren for introducing me to the important half-truth that 'all journalists are American'; Sybil Coady for her convincing number-crunching work on 'Who Was Junius?'; Dr Joseph O. Baylen for sharing with me his long years of research into the life of W. T. Stead; Charles Wintour for permitting me to quote him on one of his least favourite topics, Government by Journalism; and Harold Evans for his continuing support.

I would also like to thank the following for giving their expertise and, in many cases, material:

B. R. Bruff, The Village Press

Lida Lopes Cardozo, David Kindersley's Workshop

Terence Cockerell and colleagues, *Morning Advertiser*

Dr James Cope

Amanda Jane Doran, *Punch*

Ann Gould, Archive Graphics

Elaine Hart, *The Illustrated London News*

Ralph Hyde and colleagues, Guildhall Library

John Le Neve Johnson, The London Press Club

James Mosley and colleagues, St Bride Printing Library

Douglas Matthews and staff, The London Library

George Newkey-Burden, *The Daily Telegraph*

Canon John Oates, St Bride's Church

Brian Park and colleagues, Associated Newspapers

Gordon Phillips, The History of Advertising Trust

K. R. Pollit, Mewès & Davis

Judith Prendergast, National Portrait Gallery

Michael Roffey, Times Newspapers

Paul Rudd and colleagues, Express Newspapers

Andrew Saint, English Heritage

David Simmonds, of L. Simmonds, Fleet Street booksellers

Edmund Swinglehurst, Thomas Cook

And finally I would like also to thank Jonathan Grimwood, my publisher; Rosie Anderson, my editor, for her unstinting hard work and encouragement; and Gwyn Lewis for his sympathetic design of the book.

Foreword

Fleet Street was scooped by its own funeral. Everybody was still at lunch, it seems, when the whole colourful caravan of proprietors, editors and gossip columnists was redirected to dockland and other addresses throbbing with glamour and excitement. Those of us who were agitating in the seventies and eighties for computer typesetting were right in the prediction that it would enable more newspaper titles to flourish, but none of us imagined that this would be accompanied by such a scattering of the blots of ink.

This book is by way of a memorial service at St Bride's followed by a drink at the Press Club, with rather more of St Bride's than Lunchtime O'Booze. That is no bad thing. Lunchtime, God-bless his exes, could not improve on the truth about the Fleet Street of our times as reported by Mr Evelyn Waugh, Mr Michael Frayn, Mr Robert Harling and Mr Peter Forster. But Mr Ray Boston has entertainingly and provocatively improved our recollections of some of the historic giants of Fleet Street – Fleet Street, of course, in the sense of the national newspaper press housed between the Strand and Blackfriars, for some of them were at the peripheries of the street itself. It is good to see Thomas Barnes here, the first professional editor of *The Times*, but the last to swim from Chelsea to Westminster Bridge and the only one known to have carried a cudgel after putting the paper to bed at night in case he was set upon by diehard Tory thugs. He conformed not at all to the establishment image of the editor of *The Times*, and was all the better for it. He was a real newspaperman. He hired teams of fast horses to hurry the latest intelligence along the new turnpikes, and his pages were full of life. Then, too, there is the often-neglected W. T. Stead, who came to Fleet Street from the *Northern Echo* where the editor today is daily reminded of his duty by Stead's framed letter of appointment: 'What a marvellous opportunity for attacking the devil!' Stead invented the cross-heading, the celebrity interview, and campaigning journalism that offended the gentleman hack of his day, Matthew Arnold, just as it offends his like today in Westminster and Fleet Street (well, what other collective noun is there?). Stead was a Spiritualist who predicted the manner of his own death: he died on the *Titanic*.

I have one quarrel with Mr Boston, which is the suggestion that computerization is somehow a demon in the drama and more important commercially than journalistically. It is true that in the United States it is associated with blandly homogeneous, verbose and sprawling newspapers but that need not be. Given the unmatched craftsmanship of the Fleet Street backbenches, I doubt whether the result will be the same. The United States, after all, is mainly a monopoly press without the competitive clamour of Fleet Street, and while it has an easier time finding out what is going on it is tediously narrow in its expressions of opinion. What computerization does certainly do is give investigative journalism a chance to catch up on the facts, by the use of electronic retrieval, and clearly it has played an important part in getting all those new titles off the sketchpads. These are journalistic matters of the first importance. Nor should computerization be blamed for the decision of managements to flee south.

Still, like many others, I regret that the cursors are not flickering their impatience in Beaverbrook's brilliant black-glass palace, and that we can no longer hope to bump into the shades of Barnes and Stead, and William Cobbett and T. P. O'Connor and Hannen Swaffer and Arthur Christiansen and Sefton Delmer and James Cameron and Allen Hutt and Harold Keeble, as we hurry through the Inns of Court with a headline on our mind.

Harold Evans
New York

THE FREEDOM OF THE PRESS

Prologue

A strong impulse to rage, rather than write about old Fleet Street, came over me most powerfully one dark morning in 1988. I was walking up Bouverie Street with a colleague, musing about the 'Farewell to Fleet Street' exhibition which had just opened at the Museum of London, when our progress was halted by a heavy shower of grey-coloured gunge falling from on high. It seemed to be coming from the top floor of the new structure, rearing up aggressively where the *News of the World* once lived. We dived for shelter under the porticoed doorway of the old *Punch* offices opposite, and found ourselves staring in unison at William Hazlitt's blue plaster marker hanging on the wall beside us. It had been completely transfigured – but not in a radiance of glory! There were horrible wet splodges of cement dripping down the wall over the plaque, completely obscuring the inscription and hardening faster than glass.

It was sickening; like watching an act of vandalism in slow-motion. I was too shocked to move. Accident or no, it was an outrage! Poor old Hazlitt – not to mention poor old us! There would be no gentle farewell for *his* Fleet Street, that was clear. It was goodbye forever – and good riddance! ('Fourth Estate' indeed! 'Fourth-Rate Estate' is more like it! Wapping's too good for 'em!) I looked around wildly for the culprits. There wasn't a hard-hat in sight. There was only the mocking blare of a 'ghetto-blaster' in full cry, some way above our heads.

Nobody else seemed bothered – apart from my friend, who was shaking like an aspen leaf. 'Isn't that like life?' he queried idiotically. 'No it isn't!' I snapped, 'It's more like death! We must do something!' I was tempted to borrow a ladder from the site and wipe up the mess with my handkerchief. I knew it wouldn't do much for Hazlitt or his memorial, but it might relieve my feelings. Instead, we did precisely nothing. We were too embarrassed. We simply brushed ourselves down and went off to lunch at The Clachan.

Some hours later, while watching the main evening news on television, I thought I caught a glimpse of old Bouverie Street in the days before the exodus of the nationals began and the bulldozers moved in. I called my friend and embarked on one of our longer conversations. It was probably a production mistake, we decided, because we were shown out-of-date pictures with no trace of new building

THE DRAGON'S DISGUISE.
Lord Beaverbrook. "I WONDER IF THEY'LL SEE THROUGH THIS."

The press as others saw it: the blood-thirsty dragon trying hard to be St George. (L. Raven Hill, in *Punch*, 18 March 1931)

Opposite Fleet Street as a snake pit. Cobra-like, Beaverbrook of the *Daily Express* dominates Illingworth's spiteful, back-biting scene. The *News Chronicle* and the *Daily Herald* (which died in 1960 and 1964 respectively) eat each other savagely in the struggle to survive, while *The Sunday Times* and *The Observer* exist as two ends of the same superior snake. (*Punch*, 29 May 1957)

work in progress. But we enjoyed a lively discussion: what treasures will archaeologists find when they are scrabbling about among the ruins of this once-wealthy Wall Street-in-Europe to see what was there before? And how will anyone ever believe that Fleet Street was once a habitation of the mind, long before it was a 'Street of Adventure' or even a 'Street of Shame'? Where journalists 'lived dangerously so that others could live more fully' and 'disclosure was the principal duty of a newspaper editor'?

'Sounds like the worst excesses of the French Revolution,' said my conservative friend. 'Yes, it does,' I replied, 'Citizen Tom Paine, the 'Rights of Man', Liberty, Equality, Fraternity and all that!' But it was true enough, once upon a radical reform time. Even the editor of *The Times*, Thomas Barnes, was upset by the news of Peterloo. It has been called the Golden Age of Journalism – and not just by rheumy-eyed old hacks with one foot in the grave and one eye on the colour supplements.

The most disturbing news out of old Fleet Street these days is, of course, private and financial. It is no longer general and functional. It reads like a company report and is about as sensational as scrambled eggs. It may disturb a few businessmen occasionally. But it leaves most mainline news addicts colder than methadone. It reflects the new Fleet Street exactly: it is neat, prim and compact, and will fit comfortably into any old Filofax. But, for those who yearn for the good old days, when truly investigative journalism was available, free from deference and burning with democratic indignation, this kind of recipe lacks body as well as fire.

Old Fleet Street is old history even to Londoners. Its journalists and taverns, coffee-houses and printing presses disappeared long ago. The Fleet Street we had been walking around, comparatively freely, was largely a Northcliffe creation dating from the 1890s, with a few additions built in the 1930s. It will probably remain with us for a little while longer, visually at least. Its proximity to the Law Courts and Inns of Court will provide it with some kind of protection. But the new Fleet Street waits for no journalist, merely information of a very special kind. It is intent on a complete break with old associations. It is not just adapting itself to the new technology: it is rebuilding for an entirely different future. It will soon be seen for what it is, an international zone for stateless companies, a banking and insurance enclave for multi-national corporations. Where it will all end, knows God! But what we felt *we* knew, with some certainty, was that all trace of its old newspaper history would soon be erased from public memory – unless somebody somehow did something about it. Which is when we decided to intervene.

We have tried to bring to Fleet Street the tribute of an informed nostalgia, through simple words and pictures: to put the real past on record before the legendary past (and abuse) finally triumph. We dearly wanted to celebrate the old household gods of Liberty and Fraternity before the new ones, Enterprise and Greed, had swept everything else off the shelf.

Most people have about as substantial an idea of Fleet Street as they have of Camelot. They read histories and watch plays about it that are largely mythical.

AJAX DEFYING THE THUNDERER

The press as it liked to see itself: god-like in its omniscience and opposed to all kinds of tyranny (except the more popular forms). Sir Bernard Partridge's cartoon represented a travesty of the appeasement role of *The Times* in the years before the Second World War, when the paper was requested to recall its senior correspondent in Berlin. (*Punch*, 18 August 1937)

They seem not to care where the truth ends and the fiction begins, so long as the story is colourful. 'When the news becomes a legend, we prefer the legend!'

But underneath this veneer of so-called sophistication, there is a softwood of naive trust and simplicity. Many want desperately to believe what they read, if only because they can't always believe what they see. 'It must be because it says so, here in the paper'.

Even among the 12 million tabloid readers in Britain today, 'up to no good but the beat of their blood', there is some residual memory of what was once quoted with respect by their parents; some flicker of curiosity seeking to know what it was all about before television and the 'Three-Minute Culture'. We think it was about public service, not simply public scandal; about muck-raking for God, not just moon-raking for the Devil. Like Camelot, Fleet Street used to involve adventure and knight-errantry, as well as skullduggery. It was about putting down the mighty and uplifting the weak, not just chasing celebrities from pillow to bedpost. Reporters once spent more of their time watch-dogging the abuse of power than door-stepping the abuse of fame. To be sensational simply in order to sell newspapers was reckoned to be immoral. But to use sensationalism to draw public attention to a public 'hurt' – this was Fleet Street's forte before it became synonymous with shame.

This is what we think was meant by the term 'Fourth Estate', people power not publicity power – an idea first formulated by William Hazlitt in his famous essay on William Cobbett. Some say it will live forever in the Fifth Estate – broadcasting. Maybe – with some changes here and there. But I must not anticipate. Read yourself in. Consider first, the place as it once was, the personal forces which guided it, and the powerful forces which eventually killed it. Then, and only then, consider whether posterity might one day regret its unmourned passing into oblivion. You owe it to yourself to be your own historian as we walk backwards together into the future.

P.S. Walking up Bouverie Street, some months after the 'gunge' incident, I was not surprised to discover that one of my worst fears had already been realized. Hazlitt's plaque had been torn down, along with the wall on which it had been hanging for so many years. I was assured by the surprised site foreman (surprised that anyone cared!) that it would, of course, be replaced, 'unless it disturbs the new tenants of the new Tudor Court'. I can, however, share with you this snapshot of the original memorial, given to me with great generosity by Mr Michael Fullick, an employee of Wates the Builders. It tells the whole sad story of Fleet Street in one, and prompts an old hymn-tune overture for this book: 'Change and decay in all around I see; O Thou, who changest not, abide with me'. AMEN.

This plaque, ripped untimely from the wall of Hazlitt's former residence, lay half-forgotten in the dust for months. But developers in the vicinity of Hazlitt House in Bouverie Street have undertaken to perpetuate the memory of one of England's greatest reporters and critics, 'somewhere, somehow'.

1 The Place: Why Fleet Street?

'At the sign of the Sun': the plaque affixed by the Wynkyn de Worde Society at Stationers' Hall, off Ludgate Hill, in 1988. This site was chosen for its presumed safe distance from the development of Fleet Street. Wynkyn's printing press, transferred from Caxton's house in the grounds of Westminster Abbey in 1500, was reassembled near St Bride's, where de Worde (or Wynandus van Woerden) was buried in 1535.

Fleet Street extends eastwards from Temple Bar as far as Ludgate Circus, and 'if you work or live in the area bounded by Temple Bar, the Embankment, New Bridge Street, Farringdon Street and Holborn, St Bride's is your parish church and has been for a thousand years.' You may also like to know that St Bride's was 'the inspiration for the first tiered wedding cake, a madrigal in stone; the place of baptism for Pepys; the highest spire or steeple which Sir Christopher Wren ever built; the setting of many of the Royal Councils of "bad" King John, and the venue for the marriage of the parents of the first white child born in colonial America in 1575'.

But, if you want to know why Fleet Street became the chief location for London's news industry for nearly 500 years, you will need to look a little further than these pretty claims made on behalf of the present rector of St Bride's, Canon John Oates, by the Publicity Club of London. Why Fleet Street? Why not Westminster, where William Caxton set up the first printing press? Surely, he was closer to the fount of news than his principal assistant, Wynkyn de Worde,[1] who opened up for business independently 'at the sign of the Sun' near St Bride's Church in 1500? It is a question not easily answered. The ultimate reasons for an industry's location, like those of a city itself, can be hard to fathom. But the key to the answer seems to lie in that simple phrase, 'the fount of news'. Caxton was a most modest printer, using his press mainly for the glorification of God. He was indeed closer to the political heads of Church and State in Westminster. But he was not closer to the *real* fount of news which was money, circulating faster than ever before in the ancient commercial heartland of the City.

Money meant cash trading instead of barter. Money meant mobility and modernity. It held strong and persuasive evidence of men's real preferences, which were material rather than spiritual. Money meant manipulative power over feudal power. Money was news. Most men with money lived in the City. The position of Fleet Street, therefore, was strategic. De Worde was drawn to this mainland artery between King, Court and Church, because it was bound to be traversed repeatedly by anyone doing official business in London. It was already the centre of literacy, organized by the Knights Templar and the Carmelites of

14

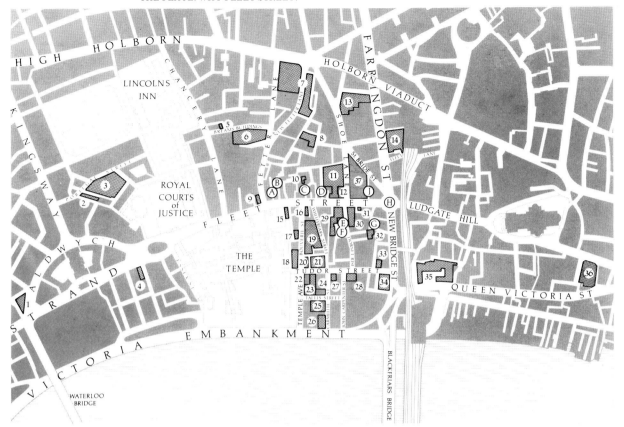

A Crane Court
B Red Lion Court
C Bolt Court
D Wine Office Court
E Salisbury Court
F Salisbury Square
G Bride Lane
H Ludgate Circus
J Poppins Court

1 *Morning Post*
2 *Church Times* and *The Financial Times*
3 W H Smith (from 1920)
4 W H Smith (before 1920)
5 *The Athenaeum*
6 *Daily Mirror* (before 1960)
7 *Daily Mirror* (since 1960)
8 Newspaper House (Westminster Press)
9 *Sheffield Daily Telegraph*
10 Bolt Court School
11 *The Daily Telegraph*
12 *Liverpool Daily Post*
13 *Evening Standard*
14 Fleetway House (Amalgamated Press)
15 *Glasgow Herald*
16 *The Scotsman*

17 *Punch*
18 *News Chronicle*
19 *News of the World*
20 *Daily News* and *The Star*
21 Northcliffe House (Associated
   Newspapers)
22 Argus Printing Company
23 Temple House (Horace Marshall
   and Sons)
24 National Press Agency
25 Carmelite House (*Daily Mail* and
   Evening News)
26 New Carmelite House
27 *The Daily Telegraph* reserve printing works
28 Co-operative Printing Society
29 *Daily Chronicle* and *Lloyd's Weekly News*
30 Reuters and Press Association
31 *Birmingham Daily Post*
32 St Bride Foundation Institute
33 Institute of Journalists
34 Blackfriars House (Spicer Brothers)
35 Printing House Square (*The Times* and
   The Observer)
36 Bracken House (*The Financial Times*
   from 1959)
37 Express Newspapers

Map showing the principal press sites in and around Fleet Street. With the exception of the *Daily Mirror* and its associates, all the national newspapers had moved away by 1990. (From Susie Barson and Andrew Saint's *A Farewell to Fleet Street*, accompanying the exhibition of that name at the Museum of London in 1988)

Whitefriars, south of the street. It was also London's main legal thoroughfare, passing close to the various Inns of Court now seeking greater prestige through printed documentation in Biblical style. Long before the coming of the first newspaper, Fleet Street and the many lanes and alleyways leading off it, up to Holborn and down to the Thames below St Paul's, had been plentifully stocked with clerks and scriveners whose livelihood depended on gathering and disseminating information, mainly about money but not exclusively.

De Worde printed nearly 800 books on his press at St Bride's and became a very wealthy man. He also made clever use of at least 17 different varieties of colophon or identifying trade mark, in all of which Caxton's initials are prominent. Why he did this, nobody knows for sure. It seems excessive purely as a mark of respect to his teacher. It is more likely to have been a coded reminder to his customers that he was well-connected despite the 'frivolity' of some of his cheaper productions. He may also have been trying to warn his executors to tread carefully when going through his literary effects for saleable material.

The last book he issued was *The Complaint of the Too-Soon Martyred* in 1535 – a book showing a distinct tendency to stray from the innocuous field of scriptural record and decoration into the more exciting (and profitable) fields of religious and political controversy. He died at the beginning of that year, but not before it had been made clear to him that some of his more infamous 'frivolities' had upset his patron, Princess Margaret, mother of Henry VII, as well as the authoritarian Tudor government in Whitehall. His printing press was confiscated and given over to Richard Pynson, a more dutiful and circumspect printer, and then to Thomas Berthelet, Printer to the King, who made it the centrepiece of the first officially recognized state printing works, built into an old monastery near Blackfriars Bridge situated on the corner of what is now Queen Victoria Street.

For the next two hundred years, this strongly guarded establishment dominated the London printing and publishing scene. It later became known as Printing House Square and was the first home of *The Times*. (The site is now occupied by Continental Bank House.) But at that time, it was concerned with 'expelling and avoiding the occasion of erroneous and seditious opinions', according to the Royal Proclamation of 1538, which covered printing of any kind. All books had to be licensed here, the Stationers' Company had representatives in the building with powers of search and seizure, and the number of master printers, apprentices and printing presses was strictly limited.

Fleet Street was separated from Blackfriars by the Fleet River which now runs under Farringdon Street and New Bridge Street. Access to it from the City side was through Ludgate and over Fleet Bridge. For many yards westwards, it was dark and swampy, heavily wooded and 'smelling evilly', presumably from the sewage in the river-moat as well as from the rotting vegetation. But in Tudor times, from Charing Cross to Blackfriars, Fleet Street was at the eastern end of a long parade of palaces, each with its own printing press as well as its own private chapel.

Artist's impression imaginatively re-created by H. W. Brewer (1895), featured in *Old London Illustrations: London in the XVI Century*. Outstanding in this medieval panorama are Ludgate, at the entrance to the City; the Fleet River, which was a major waterway spanned by a wooden bridge strong enough to carry heavily laden wagons and coaches into Fleet Street; old St Paul's with its lead-covered wooden steeple; and the high-walled Blackfriars monastery, only partially destroyed by Henry VIII at the Dissolution and replaced by the King's Printing House.

H.W. Brewer. 1895

From the palace of Bridewell at the Fleet River end (later to become a work-house and then the first women's prison in London) to Cardinal Wolsey's other and more domestic palace on the corner of Chancery Lane (later to become the first Public Record Office), most fine printers worked in virtual secrecy under aristocratic patronage. (The Savoy Palace, backing onto what is now the Strand, housed John of Gaunt, and Somerset House, built by Protector Somerset, was lived in later by Henrietta Maria, Charles I's queen.) According to Walter Thornbury in his *Old and New London* (1872): 'They operated like forgers, coun-terfeiting rare works of art, such as "La Morte d'Arthur" and "The Ship of Fools", falsifying the dedications and changing the inscriptions for posterity to puzzle over'. They were not in business for themselves, as Wynkyn de Worde had been: neither were they tied for life to one patron. They moved from palace to palace like master artists or chefs. They left the crude handbills and chapbooks to lesser mortals who needed the money and were prepared to work with the new tribe of 'newsmongers'. These dubious characters sold 'literature' as a fishmonger sold fish, collecting gossip from the four corners of London; the Court, the Church, the City and Parliament, and getting it printed as cheaply as possible. They moved into Fleet Street during the later years of Elizabeth's reign, working the royal route to St Paul's like traders in Oxford Street, making fortunes out of 'antiquated pamphlets with new dates'. They made most of their money outside the many theatres and freakshows in Whitefriars. (Whitefriars Hall, part of the old Carme-lite monastery, was turned into a theatre in the reign of James I. It was where many of Dryden's plays first appeared.) But they did not compile, compose or manufacture their 'dubious wares all invention', in Fleet Street. In Holborn (or Hollow Bourne), Aldgate, Clerkenwell even, or Cripplegate (where the name 'Grub Street' originated), but not the Fleet Street area where printers worked only for gentlemen.

Authoritative news, a scarce commodity, was produced solely by the King's Printer and his associates at Blackfriars, 'to instruct the nation in its duty and to scotch wild rumours'. Then, as now, war was the great news-maker, and one of the earliest of these official productions concerned the Battle of Flodden, 'emprynted by me Richard Faques dwllyng near poulys church-yerde on the 9th of September 1513', presumably soon after the battle. Its banner headline reads as follows: 'Hereafter ensue the trewe encountre or Batayle lately don between Englande and Scotlande'. Another interesting relic on the library shelf of official news in English is the equally rare news pamphlet (one copy disappeared with American bibliophile Harry Widener in the 1912 *Titanic* disaster) entitled: 'Hevy newes of an horryble earthquake' dated 1542.[2] This is a most confident and knowing report, concerning recent earthquakes in Europe, which has been turned into a compo-site for religious reasons. It quotes eyewitnesses in Turkey as well as Florence and Sicily, 'where the Devil lives', but it is not, strictly speaking, a newsletter, being clearly intended for inclusion in a scholarly book. However, it reads pacily enough, almost racily, as though written under pressure.

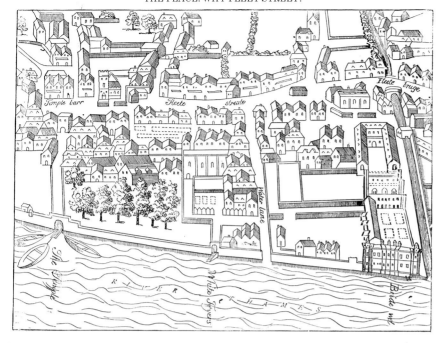

Printers and patrons, not to mention the authorities, would undoubtedly have liked to hear about the heroic exploits and triumphs of brave, Protestant Englishmen against the Catholic foreign devils. Unfortunately, the achievements of English armies throughout most of the sixteenth century, were, to say the least, disappointing, and licensed printers tended to ignore the various fiascos. Not until the 1580s, with the advent of the sea-dogs, could they give full vent to their patriotic ardour, with the sea-dogs invariably fighting against overwhelming odds and, equally invariably, emerging victorious. Contemporaries eagerly devoured accounts of a battle between 'A Ship of 200 Tun, having in her but 36. men and 2. Boyes, who were... set upon by 6 Men of Warre of the Turkes, having at least 1500. men in them', or of the encounter between 'Fyve shippes of London against xj.gallais and ij.frigates, the strongest in christendom'.

And the propaganda element was well to the fore during the excitement of the Spanish Armada, with such publications as the 'New Ballet of the straunge and most cruel Whippes which the Spanyards had prepared to Whippe and torment Englishmen and women', or the detailed account of massacre and rape, village by village, perpetrated by Spanish troops in the Netherlands. Then, as now, blood and sex reigned supreme; unusually ghastly crimes were assured of a splendid coverage, with vivid descriptions of the crime itself and (even more harrowing) of the punishment inflicted. Another type of official news concerned the Court and royal pageantry: 'Of the Tryumphe and the uses that Charles themperour & the Kyng of England were saluted with passyng through London' (1522), or, 'The Passage of most dred Soveraigne Lady Quene Elyzabeth to Westminster the day before her Coronacion' (1558).

Ralph Aggas's plan of Fleet Street, the Temple, etc., in 1563. The Knights Templar, who settled in the area, were a military and religious order set up to protect pilgrims travelling to and from the Holy Land. (From *Old Fleet Street*, in the *London Recollected* series by G. W. Thornbury, reprinted by The Village Press)

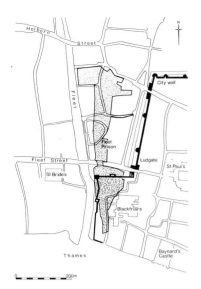

A major excavation project along the Fleet Valley began in 1988 in conjunction with the Ludgate redevelopment. The removal of the rail bridge at the foot of Ludgate Hill in 1990 gave the first uninterrupted view of St Paul's Cathedral from Fleet Street for 124 years. Finds included a wide range of relics from the Fleet Prison, Blackfriars Monastery and the City Wall. In medieval times the Fleet was a major waterway, but after the Great Fire of 1666 it became a canal and then, 100 years later, an underground sewer.

But Fleet Street and London publishers generally were suddenly seen to be lagging far behind their counterparts in Germany, not merely in fine printing but also as regards commercial news. Money news was the rage everywhere except in London, where it was frowned on by the Romish Church. Shipping news and commodity prices, revealing changing values and expanding markets overseas, suddenly mattered more than a war to the death between Protestantism and Catholicism. Spain, it was whispered, was bound to win, having more gold than anyone else in Europe as well as more men and resources. England should remain lukewarm in its support of militant Protestantism – which it did, much to the profit of the City and an impoverished Catholic monarch. By 1620, business periodicals in English were arriving in London from Amsterdam and Cologne, packed with commercial news. They were very expensive and dangerous to possess. But they were authoritative, having been authorized by the Fuggers of Augsburg and the Mandels of Frankfurt, Europe's leading bankers. They also carried human interest news, sub-titled 'Domestic News', as a sugar coating to the hard pill of business information. This might have been termed 'political', if it had not been mostly 'miracles, prodigies and wonders'.

For some dark reason, they were not very regular in their appearance, nor were they reliably translated into English. The City turned to local printers for translations, and were not disappointed. Occasionally, they came across exciting foreign news of warming-pan babies, assassinations, and even attacks on royal personages by lepers seeking the Royal Touch. No licensed printer would dare reproduce such tales, or anything which might be said to reflect on official life in London. They also had to be careful not to add anything to these foreign imports which were officially monitored. Thomas Archer, a Fleet Street bookseller operating in a side street off Fetter Lane, was given a long and painful prison sentence for publishing corantos without licence at this time. His real offence seems to have been 'making up, or adding to, his foreign corrantos': accurate translations were apparently acceptable, since, according to a letter of the period cited by Frank, 'now there is another that hath got a license to print corrantos and sell them, *honestly* translated out of the Dutch' [my italics].

This new printer, 'N.B.', was undoubtedly Nicholas Bourne, publisher of *The Courant or Weekly Newes* which first appeared for sale on the steps of Old St Paul's on 9 October, 1621. He is sometimes confused with the best-known of his many writers, transcribers and translators, Nathaniel Butter, who compiled *News from Spain* in 1611, printed and published at his own expense. Bourne ran a large print shop near the Royal Exchange in direct competition with Thomas Archer. He employed Butter to translate foreign news and collect local gossip, circulating it in handwritten letters to gentlemen, by word of mouth and handbill to theatre crowds, as well as through the printing press in officially licensed newspapers. Bourne, not Butter, was legally responsible for the *Weekly Newes* over the next thirty years, and it seems to have been Bourne's decision to translate foreign newsletters, simply, regularly and in their full entirety, thus making them the forerunners of general interest newspapers like *The Daily Courant* (1702) rather than of purely commercial newspapers like *Lloyd's News* (1696).

Butter was a law unto himself, operating without any patron except the mob, and must have been quite a character. He worked, 'fitfully', as a scrivener in the Alienation Office (now 3 Inner Temple and a canteen for law students), built in 1577 by Robert Dudley, Earl of Leicester, 'for all things foreign or estranged that do come to us'. For 'fitfully' read 'freelance', because by all accounts he was the busiest vendor of printed news in London. He is referred to as 'a decayed stationer' in Ben Jonson's *The Staple of Newes* (1625) and is publicly reviled for manufacturing 'news-bait for fishes to be caught'. The source for most of his news, said Jonson, was 'The Man in the Moon'. Like the famous Charlie Hand who worked for the *Daily Mail* from its inception to his death, Butter was a specialist in theatre gossip and had a most sensitive nose for royal news. It is said he could distract a large crowd with his newsmongering patter. He spoke Cockney and 'dressed like Tarleton', the most popular comedian of his day. But Jonson, second in esteem only to Shakespeare when Butter first began his news enterprise, complained bitterly about his stale news: 'How he cheats upon the Time! By Buttering o'er again once in seven years, His antiquated pamphlets with new dates'. He also detested Butter's presumption: 'It is the poet who feigns a Commonwealth and governs it with counsels!' – not a low usurper of both stage and pulpit. Even so, he could not help but admire Butter's verbal skill at 'angling his wares into novelties' when talking to theatre crowds. 'Protestant News and Pontifical News, Authenticall and Apocryphal, Tailors' News and Traitors' News, Porters' and Watermen's News' – these were some of his 'come-ons', according to Jonson. 'The expectation of the vulgar is more drawn and held with newness than with goodness. So be it new, though never so naught and depraved, they run to it and are taken, poor fools!' (According to John Gore in *The Ghosts of Fleet Street* (1928), 'Jonson used the Devil's Tavern at 1, Fleet Street as his London office, when writing his plays.')

But Jonson was fighting a losing battle. In 1642, only six years after his death, the theatres were closed and public discussion was channelled henceforth into the newspaper press. In 1645, more than 700 different news sheets appeared. The poet dramatist had indeed lost his vocation – or so it seemed. But cold figures do not tell the whole story: more significant is the fact that newsbooks never enjoyed the full support of government. They were tolerated for almost a decade, while business was booming and the war news was favourable. But, on 17 October 1632, the newsbooks were abruptly suppressed. According to Butter, the news from the Continent had been so bad 'that the Lords would not have it known'. For the next six years, repression was the order of the day, with the Star Chamber decree of 1637 laying down the most detailed rules yet for the regulation of the Press – partly, perhaps, as a result of the Archbishop's fury at the errors in the official printing of the 1631 edition of the Bible, in which Exodus 20:14 read, 'Thou shalt commit adultery', and Deuteronomy 5:24, 'The Lord hath shewed us his glory and his great asse'. Blasphemy as well as sedition was thought to be inherent in the printing press.

In 1638, the old firm of Butter and Bourne, backed by a syndicate of ambitious merchants, once again petitioned the King for a renewal of their privilege to publish translations of foreign business news. To their surprise, they were awarded a monopoly, which was almost like a licence to print money. They were forbidden to sell in the streets or even in the taverns, but no limit was placed on what they might charge for private subscriptions. They, naturally, revived their old title of *Weekly Newes* and, according to Butter, 'prospered mightily' for the next two years until their royal monopoly was revoked by the Long Parliament. Butter survived, somehow, until 1644: by which time, Fleet Street had been transformed from a stately thoroughfare of shops, theatres and palaces, into 'an evill-smelling warren of vile profit and sedition'. Plague and pestilence may explain the first part of Butter's malediction, 'Universally death is in London, and most about The Temple and Fleet Street,' but not the second half which reflects his personal disgust at the 'new pornographie' which was everywhere in print at the time of his death.

Civil war had encouraged licentiousness as well as lawlessness. Authority was

The origins of the Fleet Prison, on the eastern bank of the Fleet River, date back to at least the twelfth century. It was rebuilt several times following riots and finally in the 1780s following the Gordon Riots. When this impression appeared in 1858, the site had been cleared but the railway viaduct, closed in 1990 and later demolished, had only just been erected.

divided not merely between Oxford and Westminster, but also between the City of London and Westminster. Fleet Street had become a no-man's land outside the City walls. Street fights between local gangs was a daily occurrence, until the military actually appeared to interrupt them, *en route* to the river and the military transports anchored there. Even the night watch was abandoned, according to Pepys: garbage filled the single ditch running down the middle of the street, and 'fires after dark, which were frequent, were left to themselves'. 'Alsatia was the name given to this no-man's land, after the name of the ever-troubled country between France and Germany.' It quickly became a sanctuary for all the rowdies in London, much to the fear and annoyance of the stern legal gentlemen of the Temple. 'The latter once tried to brick up the entrance to the Temple at the end of what is now Tudor Street, but the "Alsatians" would have none of it, undoing the work of the masons as soon as they built it up'.[3] Theatres became barracks with stabling, taverns 'open brothels', and churches storehouses for gunpowder, according to Thornbury, who also talks disapprovingly of 'Fleet Street marriages' as a 'new business for Fleet Street taverners at this time'. They were performed illegally by debt-imprisoned clerics on parole from the nearby Fleet Prison.

Respectable booksellers tended to support Parliament while hoping for a reconciliation, talking vaguely about 'the malignant party' and 'the bloody-minded cavaliers' in newsbooks filled mostly with foreign business news. These were produced in bookshops and print-shops grouped around the old Exchange and the Old Bailey. Fleet Street publishers, on the other hand, supported nobody but themselves, as opportunists always do.

They accepted contracts from anyone with a good idea and discovered there were huge profits to be made out of human interest items about the King and the Royal Family. These suddenly became available, for copying and embroidering, when the first Royalist newsbook of any consequence, *Mercurius Aulicus or Court Journal*, reached London from Oxford in January 1643. Edited by Sir John Berkenhead, King Charles's propaganda minister, and printed on an old Caxton press in Oriel College, *Aulicus* was intended to be a rabble-rousing production and succeeded beyond all expectations. It was hugely entertaining as well as 'sonorously sentimental about the Royal Family; personal to the point of viciousness about Parliamentary leaders and generally scornful of any kind of authority except that of the King. Simply written and expensively produced, it sold for much less than was customary for a newsbook. It was, of course, heavily subsidized by Royalist sympathizers. It was clearly intended to subvert and was smuggled regularly through the Parliamentary lines to London, sometimes by friendly watermen of the Thames, sometimes by secret agents, and once by the French Ambassador who was caught red-handed with a dozen copies as he passed through Temple Bar on his way home to Blackfriars from Westminster. Thus began one of the liveliest periods in the history of the press.

'In times of this nature, it is not good to hold arguments, only to ask questions,' begins one issue of *Aulicus*. Listed as 'London Lyes', these were crammed with

Temple Bar, with its dusty galleries high above the street lined with chained books and documents, survived *in situ* until 1878, when it was removed to (and still remains derelict in) Theobalds Park. The City boundary at this point is still marked by a fabulous beast or stone griffin, traditionally supposed to be capable of guarding gold in any form. (From *Old Fleet Street*, in the *London Recollected* series by G. W. Thornbury, reprinted by The Village Press)

innuendo and much too provocative to be ignored. There had to be some kind of official answer at the same level of verbal viciousness – and when it came, entitled *Mercurius Britannicus or The People's Paper*, the first major press war began in Fleet Street. Typical of the exchanges that now ensued was that sparked off by a report in *Aulicus* on 23 December 1643 that a prisoner of the Royalists had been found committing buggery on a mare – and on a Sunday, of all days, when 'His Majestie's Forces were all at Church'. *Britannicus* responded to this 'foul calumny' by claiming that the soldier in question had merely been trying to steal the horse in order to escape, and he very much doubted if any Royalist soldiers had been to church 'since his Majestie first levied war against his Parliament'. If they had, he continued, it would have been to attend mass![4]

The battle between *Aulicus* and *Britannicus* (edited by Marchamont Nedham, a lawyer's clerk at Gray's Inn, and printed by Thomas Newcombe in Thames Street, over against Baynard's Castle) continued strongly until October 1645, when *Aulicus* ceased without explanation and *Britannicus* lost its chief *raison d'être*. Both reappeared eventually, but in the interval Mercuries became available all over London, issuing from every alleyway in Fleet Street, with 'little more than Billingsgate language in any of them'. The old-style newsbooks produced around the old Exchange tended to keep out of this mêlée and so lacked sales and general circulation. But they prospered nevertheless, because they carried news of battle casualties unobtainable anywhere else. By early 1644, a dozen appeared in London every week. According to Joseph Frank, the minimum circulation was about 200 copies, with well-established newsbooks selling 500, and *A Perfect Diurnall*, 'reliable if pedestrian,' between 750 and 1,000 (the same estimate as for the far more lively *Mercurius Britannicus*).

Such figures may well be exaggerated. This was no time for honest trading; survival was more important. Fleet Street had discovered that exploiting the really grand passions at home paid much better than pandering to small private ones abroad. The Mercuries, like modern tabloids, were hugely popular. They were sold openly in the streets by licensed Mercury women as well as by unlicensed hawkers. They were 'full of lies, forgeries, insolencies and impieties', derived largely from one-line hints in *Aulicus*. They were also compulsively written and may have driven many people to learn to read in order to gain some social advantage over cowed and ignorant neighbours. But nobody cared, except the authorities. 'For Mercuries, like committees, will beget one another,' noted Berkenhead in his Oxford stronghold, fully aware that he was causing a social problem as well as a journalistic problem for the Parliamentary authorities in London. 'My aim,' he said, somewhat lacking in frankness, 'was to create laughter rather than dismay,' and this he achieved by 'bawdry and smut' at a time when public morality was a major concern of the government. His great talent for 'black' propaganda put him head and shoulders above the crowd of 'hackney, factionalist scribblers' employed on each side during the Civil War, and perhaps his greatest coup was persuading Nedham, the chief writer and editor of *Britannicus*, to defect to the Royalists in the summer of 1647, bringing his Fleet Street skills and inside information with him to Oxford. After the execution of the King in 1649, Nedham was unlucky enough to be captured: he escaped, was recaptured, imprisoned for some months, and finally re-emerged in Fleet Street at a time when desperate attempts were being made to stamp out anything and everything which even remotely resembled the journalism of the Royalist press, as decreed by the Chief Censor, John Milton. They included, interestingly enough, John Lilburne's *Petition of the Levellers for a Free Press*, published in Fleet Street in 1649. Berkenhead, meanwhile, had become a secret agent on the Continent for the future King Charles II. The antiquary Anthony à Wood got him right when he called him 'this seditious, unstable and railing author'.

The Restoration, contrary to the popular myth starring Nell Gwynn and the Merry Monarch, together with later, semi-fictional composites like Moll Flanders, was an even bleaker period for Fleet Street. It was not a case of change your partners for a merry dance; it was simply more of the same thing – repression. Charles II and James II ran a very tight media policy, using all the traditional machinery of repression plus a few refinements of their own learned in France. These included the supervision by secretaries of state of all incoming information and the services of a new Surveyor of the Press with draconian powers of search. Temporarily, the newsbook languished. But in its place there flourished that other direct ancestor of the modern newspaper, the *written* newsletter, or 'Quality Street' news-sheet.

Newsletters had long existed as private sources of information among the wealthy and influential. They covered the daily events at Court in precise detail and were deemed essential reading because of the rapid changes of the royal mood and, therefore, of the political pecking order. They now assumed a far greater importance, partly because of the control exercised over printed news and partly because of improvements in the postal services. In 1649, the original weekly post from London had been augmented by a second post, and a third was added in 1655, so that letters could be posted on Tuesdays, Thursdays and Saturdays to any sizeable town in the country.

Cromwell's anti-press laws were strictly enforced right up to his death. But handwritten letters had been controlled only by the very high postal rates. Again, it was royal authority which first grasped the possibilities of the newsletter as a news controller. Charles II wished to disseminate certain carefully authenticated news to influential persons in every part of the kingdom. He also wanted information for his own purposes. Cheaply printed news, he was advised, would be dismissed as ephemeral trash. But expensive newsletters on fine paper would naturally be limited to 'the right people' and would remain confidential, especially if they were officially stamped, handwritten, personally addressed and personally angled. These would be much more acceptable than 'a printed rag'! And so it proved when the government set up an elaborate intelligence system based on the well-known and trusted newsletter of Henry Muddiman.[5]

According to James Sutherland in his exhaustive study, *The Restoration Newspaper and its Development*, published in 1986, Muddiman (1629–92) sent out all his signed newsletters from his own office at the Seven Stars in the Strand, but he invariably headed them 'Whitehall'. The fact that many of the officially-paid replies that he received are now among the State Papers indicates that he passed them on to under-Secretary Sir Joseph Williamson, who had been his patron for many years. Other letters were addressed to the under-Secretary but marked, 'For Mr. Henry Muddiman'. That Muddiman was asking for and receiving information from some if not all of the subscribers to his expensive newsletter (£5 per year) may be instanced by a reply he received from William Duckett, member of Parliament for Calne in Wiltshire, beginning: 'Sir, In your last you desired me to acquaint you what nonconformists, papists and others were indicted at quarter sessions...'

Muddiman continued to send out his handwritten newsletters until 1689. And even when the 'quality' newspaper press had greatly expanded in the reign of Queen Anne (1702–14), many gentlemen preferred to subscribe to a private newsletter because it was a personal service, giving the recipient the pleasant feeling that he was reading his own private correspondence from London. Muddiman's special printing privileges, however, granted to him in 1660 to produce an official publication called *Mercurius Publicus*, ended in 1663 when he was forced to make way for a newly-appointed Surveyor of the Press. Roger L'Estrange, a conservative fanatic, had managed to convince the King that even the Stationers' Company was not to be trusted and was harbouring some disloyal printers in their ranks. He also had very definite opinions about news: 'I think it makes the Multitude too familiar with the actions and counsels of their superiors, too pragmatical and censorious, and gives them not only an itch but a kind of colourable right to be meddling with the government.' Gossip was preferable to news, he insisted, because it could be made to bind people together 'happily', in spheres of special interest such as the Royal Family. News was divisive and destructive of general happiness, because it was open to interpretation. It was largely responsible for the alienation of the City from the King's ministers and should, therefore, be much more rigorously controlled. He requested and was granted a patent for the exclusive publication of 'all narratives or relations not exceeding two sheets of paper, and all advertisements, mercuries, diurnals and books of public intelligence, all ballads, plays, maps, charts, portraitures and pictures not previously printed, and all briefs for collections, playbills, quack-salvers' bills, customs and excise bills, post office bills, creditors' bills and tickets, in England and Wales, and with power to search for and seize unlicensed and treasonable, schismatical and scandalous books and papers'. Muddiman's business newsbooks were immediately replaced by *The Intelligencer, Published for the Satisfaction and Information of the People* on Mondays, and *The Newes* (a gossip sheet) on Thursdays.

In his prospectus, issued from the King's Printing Office in Blackfriars in August 1663, L'Estrange gave details of his licensing and inquisitorial plans, as

26

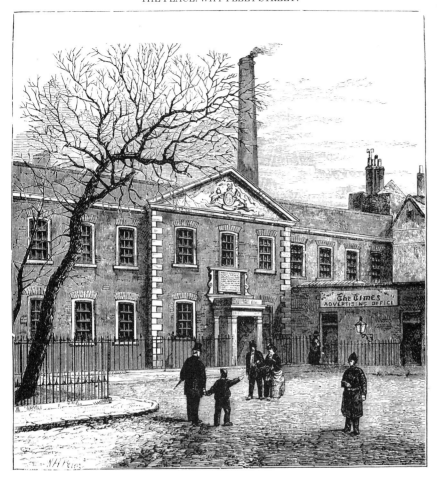

well as of his own editorial ideal. He had discovered, he said, that there were far more printers in London than the law allowed. 'I find it in general, with the printers as with their neighbours, there are too many of the trade to live by one another. But, more particularly, I find them clogged with three sorts of people – foreigners, persons not free of the trade, and separatists.' He invited all honest citizens to help him in his reforming work. Whoever brought him information leading to proof about 'any printing press erected and being in a private place, hole or corner, contrary to the tenor of the late act of parliament' should receive a reward of 40*s.*, 'with what assurance of secrecy himself shall desire'. To anyone who gave similar proof of a seditious and unlicensed book being in the press, and rendered 'his aid to the seizing of the copies and the offenders', he offered a reward of £5, and, among other bribes, one of 5*s.* for anyone helping to convict the hawker of an unlicensed book, pamphlet or newspaper. Even *The Intelligencer* or *The Newes*, if anyone desired to buy his own copy, must be procured from the King's Printing and Publishing Office, or from an 'accredited and respectable agent'. He wanted total control and he got it. Londoners could not resist such glittering

Printing House Square, formerly the King's Printing House and, before that, Blackfriars Monastery, was the home of *The Times* from 1785 until 1974. (From *Cheapside and St Paul's*, in the *London Recollected* series by G. W. Thornbury, reprinted by The Village Press)

prizes and there is no doubt about his success as an Inquisitor.

'It is on record,' says H. R. Fox Bourne, 'that one October evening in 1663, acting on information received, L'Estrange proceeded with four assistants to the house of a seditious printer named John Twyn in Cloth Fair, Holborn' (near Little Britain, where Benjamin Franklin trained to be a printer). According to one of the assistants' evidence, they knocked for at least half an hour before they got in, it being long past midnight, and while they waited, 'heard some papers tumbling down and a loud rattling above'. Admitted at length, they were in time to seize some type that had been broken up and some sheets which had not been destroyed, 'setting forth the monstrous doctrine that "the execution of judgment and justice is as well the people's as the magistrate's duty, and if the magistrates prevent judgment, the people are bound by the law of God to execute judgment without them and upon them"'.' Here, it was thought, was enough criminality to arraign Twyn before the King's Bench. The jury quickly found him guilty and the sentence was that he 'be hanged by the neck, cut down before he was dead, shamefully mutilated, and his entrails taken out. With you still living, the same to be burnt before your eyes, your head to be cut off, and your head and quarters to be disposed of at the pleasure of the king's majesty.' 'I humbly beseech your lordship,' the printer cried, 'to remember my poor condition and family and intercede for me.' 'I would not intercede for my own father in this case if he were alive,' was the judge's rejoinder. Twyn was led back to Newgate Prison (where the Old Bailey now stands) and later hurried to Tyburn (at Marble Arch) where the main portion of the sentence was carried out, his head and fragments of his body being afterwards set up 'on Ludgate, Aldersgate, and the other gates of the City', as 'an example to all men who advocate death or disobedience to such a monarch'.

Other victims were found by L'Estrange, though none were quite so cruelly used as Twyn. For example, Francis Smith, printer and publisher of *Smith's Protestant Intelligence*, went to Newgate for two years for confessing 'he would never leave writing news till he had reduced this kingdom to a commonwealth'. But L'Estrange's career as a newspaper monopolist ended as abruptly as it began, shortly before the horrendous and almost total destruction of Fleet Street in the Great Fire of 1666. When bubonic plague broke out in London in 1665, 'with a viciousness like never before', the Court shifted to Oxford. L'Estrange remained in London to enforce the licensing system, while Muddiman found himself being summoned to Oxford to edit the *Oxford Gazette*, due to become the *London Gazette* when the Court moved back again. L'Estrange tried to produce his *Publick Intelligence* without any proper staff and without any official news. He failed lamentably and was compensated with a royal pension, to be paid by Muddiman out of the profits of the *Gazette*. The Court returned to London in January 1666. Public opinion, as expressed in Parliament, was distinctly hostile towards the monarchy, particularly for its long desertion of the capital. L'Estrange's monopoly had been broken, but he remained Surveyor of the Press. In the field of news, the *London Gazette* now reigned supreme, though it was hardly an exciting publication and

was frequently criticized on this ground – until the Great Fire of September 1666 made it essential reading for everybody still alive.

A curate at St Bride's Fleet Street, Paul Boston by name, saw the old Church destroyed completely, soon after his institution on 21 August 1666 ('to be precise, only a fortnight before its destruction on September 2, 1666'). It had only recently been restored and its rebuilding, he says, was not completed till October 1703. In 1886, a contemporary letter addressed to Lord Conway, vividly describing the event, was discovered in the Public Record Office in Chancery Lane. It seems 'the flames destroyed most of Fleet Street and all the Inner Temple till it came to the Hall where it was most happily quenched, as likewise in Fleet Street over against St Dunstan's Church. Houses in the Strand, adjoining Somerset House, were blown up, so great was the despair.' Butter's old office, the Alienation Office in the Inner Temple, was completely gutted, leaving only the façade, and 'every one of the palaces, including part of the Bridewell, were rebuilt more modestly as town houses'. But one of the biggest disasters from the point of view of the Surveyor of the Press was the destruction of the King's Printing House at Blackfriars. It was not merely his centre of operations for public information control; it was his main repository for betrayal information regarding illegal printing in England and Wales, and the symbol of royal power over the press. Not surprisingly, when the *Gazette* emerged from the smoking embers of London under the imprint of L'Es-

Fleet Street was the first highway west out of the City of London to be fully restored after the Great Fire, but this building at the junction with Fetter Lane (as well as the massive Temple Bar beyond) was for many years a stubborn obstacle to the ever-increasing flow of traffic.

trange once more, it was forced to announce, alongside much sadder news, the temporary abandonment of State trials. 'In the meantime, advertisements will be received at the Intelligence Offices upon the Royal Exchange, and next door to the Pigeon Tavern, near Charing Cross. Complaints rectified on application to Mr Roger L'Estrange in Gifford's Buildings, Holborn.'

It was the beginning of a new era: deference to divine right had been put very much into question by this Act of God, along with the depositions of all those who blindly supported it. The Great Fire was seen to be a watershed, not merely in the history of London but also in the history of monarchy. London would have to be rebuilt by Londoners, that was clear. The King had no money and seemed hardly to care what happened to the City or its inhabitants once the fire had been stopped. It had obliged him, he said, to accept a pension from the King of France in order to 'live of his own', which is what he and his brother James were determined to do. Consequently, Joshua Marshall, the King's Mason, was not generally contracted by the City Fathers, as had been expected; and not even the great Sir Christopher Wren was going to dictate how London should be rebuilt. He could – and did – design most of the new churches, but his plans for a grand east-west avenue dominated by the new St Paul's were totally ignored. It was going to be 'business as usual', as quickly and as cheaply as possible.

Public interest in what was really going on outside the pages of the *London Gazette* first manifested itself in a pronounced expansion of coffee-houses, mainly in Fleet Street. From the very first one in 1652, they had been centres of news and gossip. They now began to provide specially written house newsletters, based largely on private subscription newsletters, which were increasingly critical of the government. Nando's coffee-house (1656), 'the second coffee-house in London', was rebuilt after the Fire 'in a space only ten feet wide but five storeys high', at 14 Fleet Street (numbering replaced signs from 1657). It was very popular with lawyers and was frequented regularly by Lord Chancellor Thurlow, according to E. W. Padwick (1980). 'He went there for more than coffee, it is said, being a womaniser as well as a great talker.' By the mid-1670s, when Fleet Street's rebirth was finally completed (it was not rebuilt again in its entirety until 1914), there were at least six coffee-houses in the area catering to all classes and providing attractive news-readers for groups who 'could not or would not read'.

Charles II detested the coffee-house trade and frequently tried to stamp it out as a source of sedition, even though it was in the very first London coffee-house in St Michael's Alley (1652) that his own Restoration had been schemed. In 1675, a Royal Proclamation called for the suppression of all coffee-houses as being 'places where the disaffected meet and spread scandalous reports concerning the conduct of His Majesty and his Ministers.' But, according to Bryant Lillywhite (1963), 'the public uproar which followed, soon caused the order to be withdrawn'. Coffee-house culture was much too important to the City, and to Londoners generally, to be given up without a struggle. It was liberating for the culture-starved businessman, relaxing for the off-duty lawyer, and most stimulating for the speculative

Nos. 17 and 16 Fleet Street, and between them the arched entrance to Middle Temple Lane. No. 17 is most certainly an ancient structure, but the claim on the façade in this 1899 view that it was the former palace of Henry VIII is spurious. No. 16 housed Groom's Coffee-House for many years, Nando's was at No. 14, and The Rainbow was at No. 15 behind it.

journalist, releasing him from total dependency on official sources for saleable, functional news. It dominated both the spoken and the written word for the next 200 years. It was particularly important during the French Revolution when Tom Paine replaced Dr Johnson as the main talk-show host. It only began to fade 'about 1858,' when (according to journalist Cyrus Redding) 'the rage for clubs in Pall Mall, closer to the Court and Westminster than Fleet Street, brought ruin to coffee-houses everywhere'. The Popish Plot could not have been so successfully exploited in London had it not been for these popular meeting-places. And, with the exposure of that plot, organized dissent rose to fever pitch, both inside and outside Parliament. The King was forced to prorogue his Parliament in May 1679, before the press licensing regulations could be renewed. Accidentally, therefore, the press suddenly found itself free – and made the most of its opportunity.

A number of unlicensed newspapers appeared 'from holes in the ground', published, like the official *Gazette*, twice a week. Names of the 'authors' involved were given prominence for the first time, as though everybody was fearless: these included Langley Curtiss, Francis Smith, Henry Care, Thomas Vile, Richard Baldwin and Richard Janeway. But the first to appear, on 7 July 1679, was *The Domestick Intelligence; or, News from both City and Country*, printed and published in Fleet Street by Benjamin Harris, a well-known and very successful bookseller, 'with the assistance of Nathaniel Crouch'. As the title indicated, the emphasis fell on local news. It was a well-written, boldly political news-sheet, pro-Parliament or 'Whig' as the new expression had it, Protestant to a fault, and clearly designed to further excite the passions of those already excited by the Popish Plot in the winter of 1678-9. It was an immediate success and set the pattern for most other papers that followed between 1679 and 1682, when the crack-down returned in full force.

On 26 August, when Harris had published No. 15 of his *Domestick Intelligence*, another *Domestick Intelligence* appeared on the streets, apparently identical with his own except that this one was 'printed for N.T.'.

The man who had played this scurvy 'spoiler' trick on Harris was Nathaniel Thompson, known in the trade as 'Popish Nat'. On 2 September (No. 17) Harris warned the public about the impostor: 'There has stoln into the World a Nameless Pamphlet under the Title of the Domestick Intelligence.' He went on to say that it was the work of a base and scandalous person, 'who has been Tenant to most of the prisons in and about London', and that there was 'no Real Domestick Intelligence but what is printed by Benjamin Harris, who was the first Contriver and Promoter thereof'. On 5 September, Thompson gave his own impudent version of what had happened: 'There hath lately dropt into the World an Abortive Birth (some fifteen days before the legitimate issue) by a factious, Infamous and Perjured Anti-Christian.' He continued to produce his deliberate copy and Harris was forced to change his title to *The Protestant (Domestick) Intelligence*, which left him dangerously exposed. Harris managed to steer clear of watchful authority until he published an anti-Catholic pamphlet, *An Appeal from the Country to the City*, attacking the Duke of York and advocating the claims of the King's illegitimate son, the Protestant Duke of Monmouth, to the throne.

On 5 February 1680, Harris was sentenced to a year's imprisonment, to stand in a specially erected pillory outside his own shop, and to pay a fine of £500. His day in the pillory was something of a personal triumph. The friends that he had counted on to stand by him (which included Commons members, Mercers from the City, and 'every tradesman in Fleet Street') turned up in sufficient numbers 'and would permit nothing to be thrown at him'. But no one came forward to pay his huge fine. Unwilling to sell his business, he spent the next two years in the King's Bench Prison at Southwark. He had asked to be sent to Newgate so that he could supervise his printer wife and her assistant Nathaniel Crouch, but this was refused. In desperation, he turned informer and fled to America via Bristol, with sufficient capital to open a combined coffee and bookshop in Boston 'at the corner of State and Washington streets'.[6]

Here he succeeded against formidable opposition. There were seven booksellers in his neighbourhood when he began. He sat down and wrote a spelling book that was 'a best seller in America for many years'. He published books for a distinguished clientele and thus acquired a respect and prestige that some of his rivals lacked. Between 1689 and 1692 his imprint appeared on a number of official publications for the State of Massachusetts and his was the only coffee-shop in the city 'where respectable women were to be seen'. But his progressive views were only acceptable in conversation, not in print. On 25 September 1690, his four-page, unlicensed newspaper, *Publick Occurrences, Both Foreign and Domestick*, appeared for one issue only. It was prevented from continuing because it offended the powerful clergy and criticized colonial policy (for the bad treatment of the Indians), contrary to British licensing restrictions imposed everywhere in 1662. Not for another 14 years was there a newspaper in the American colonies, and when one did appear, it was very careful to avoid Harris's simple and direct boldness. Fleet Street radicalism was too hot to handle, being associated with infamy as well as sedition. It would take a revolution to change the latter. But not even Tom Paine, personal friend of both Thomas Jefferson and George Washington, was able to deny the infamy when he attempted to democratize the American press at the end of the eighteenth century.

2   Business Forces

Benjamin Harris returned from America to Fleet Street in 1695, to take advantage of the final lapse of the Licensing Act. He was not welcomed, and in consequence was not very successful. Initially, the coffee-house market was completely closed to him and he was forced to make a living by pirating the almanacs of John Partridge, the astrologer. He also found that the public preferred expensively produced tri-weekly publications, printed in script type to imitate the handwritten newsletter, to the old once-weekly 'summary' journal. Things had certainly changed during his 12-year exile.

But Macaulay's assertion that 'English literature was now emancipated, and emancipated for ever from the control of government,' would have raised a hollow laugh among those journalists and publishers who continued to be arrested, tried, convicted and sentenced to fines, imprisonment or the pillory. What had happened was that, after 1695, everyone was free to publish what he pleased – and to take the consequences. In practice, the freedom conferred by the lapse of the Licensing Act was conditional on not publishing anything that was held to be 'improper, mischievous or illegal', and that meant anything that might be considered dangerous to 'the preservation of peace and good order of government and religion'. Some satirical verses, written in 1732 for the *Grub Street Journal*, put the true situation fairly enough:

> What means this change? The sum of all the story's,
> Tories deprest are Whigs, and Whigs in power are Tories.

When Harris did finally get started in 1699, on money borrowed at 'cruel' rates of interest, his *London Post* managed to last six years (with some help from Daniel Defoe), coming out regularly on Mondays, Wednesdays and Fridays, 'serving two-day old news spiced with temerity'. He also adopted the new custom of issuing 'postscripts' which were either printed or handwritten in Fleet Street coffee-houses. These were the forerunners of the modern stop-press column, containing fresh news that had arrived too late to be included in the printed issue of the paper. The earliest known postscript was in 1695 to the *Post-Boy* which in 1702 carried a note advertising the new feature: 'This is to give Notice that the Post-

Boy, with a written P.S. containing all the Domestick Occurrences together with the Translation of the Foreign News that arrives after the Printing of the said Post-Boy, is to be had only of Mr John Shank at Nandoes's Coffee-House, between the two Temple Gates: and at Mr Abel Roper's at the Black Boy over against St Dunstan's Church in Fleet Street' (later to become known as Peele's Coffee-House, on the corner of Fetter Lane).

Harris might have lasted much longer in the 'dangerous' business if he had given up news entirely and gone in for an opinionated weekly 'book review' publication like *Mist's Weekly Journal*. He might even have been able to persuade Daniel Defoe to let him serialize one of his rattling good yarns, like his successor William Heathcote did with *Robinson Crusoe* in the revived *London Post* of 1719. This way, at least, he would have been able to avoid the new Stamp Duty, which came into effect on 1 August 1712. All newspapers, except the official *London Gazette*, immediately raised their prices and, in consequence, many went to the wall. There is only a sarcastic reference to 'Honest Ben' as 'a salesman of quack medicines in Fleet Street' in 1713; with that, the record on Harris appears to close.

Fleet Street was now largely in the hands of the coffee trade and the book trade.

Fleet Street and the Temple, from a map published in 1720. (From *Old Fleet Street*, in the *London Recollected* series by G. W. Thornbury, reprinted by The Village Press)

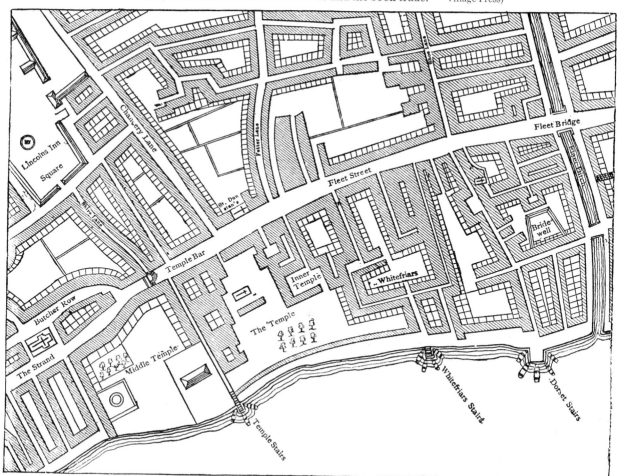

By 1750, all the leading London newspapers (which meant those carrying news at a price acceptable to most London coffee-houses) were owned by small joint-stock companies. The trend seems to have started with the first (expensive to produce) daily, *The Daily Courant*. Written by Samuel Buckley, a good linguist and a fluent writer, *The Daily Courant* (printed in Little Britain) 'prospered mightily' from the moment it first appeared in Elizabeth Mallet's bookshop on Fleet Bridge on 11 March 1702. It was to survive for 33 years, providing fresh foreign and port news daily with very little comment of any kind, at least during its early years. Later, it was to become a paper of Whig comment and ended its days as a subsidized organ of the Whig administration. It was to have no daily competitor until the foundation of the *Daily Post* (1719–46) and the *Daily Journal* (1721–37). When the *Post-Boy* became a daily in 1728, London had four so-called 'general' newspapers appearing Monday to Saturday. (There were to be no Sunday papers till 1780). Two mainly advertising papers, *The Daily Advertiser* and *The London Daily Post and General Advertiser*, followed in 1730 and 1734, and in 1735 the government of the day transferred its subsidized journalists to a new paper, *The London Gazetteer*. These three papers survived into the last decade of the eighteenth century.

Writing to Lord Godolphin in 1708, Daniel Defoe reported that *The Daily Courant* (circulation 800) was run by a club of 20 booksellers, 'whose aim is to gain of it'. So too, in 1719, Hugh Meere, the Holborn printer, testified that the 'author' of the *Daily Post* was employed by several Fleet Street booksellers, and that he had heard 'some [members] of the Play-House are also concerned therein'. In February 1728, when the masters of various coffee-houses objected to the *Daily Journal* raising its price, 'some of the proprietors of that thriving newspaper met them in the Devil Tavern, at No. 1 Fleet Street, and agreed to return to the price of $1\frac{1}{2}d$' (worth more than a £1 in modern currency, according to Roy Jenkins). The fact that they called such a meeting would seem to indicate that the *Daily Journal* was one of those most in demand by customers and that, more often than not, several copies would be required each day in each establishment. It also demonstrates the importance of a good sale in the coffee-house, and may even explain why 'the creation of a newspaper establishment, interested in investment returns, not innovation' (Michael Harris, 1978), produced stagnation in journalistic enterprise at the political level.

'Governments will not be jested with, nor reflected upon', Defoe had noted in his *Review* in 1704. 'Learn this and you will prosper.' The proper place to discuss grievances, in his view, was Parliament and not the press. The 1688 Bill of Rights had made no mention of the freedom of the press, insisting that 'the freedom of speech and debate in Parliament ought not to be impeached or questioned in any court or place out of Parliament'. For Defoe, and most other businessmen, the business of the press was business. Ministers were no more ready than kings to allow their actions to be criticized in newspapers. Advertisements rather than advocacy was the road to affluence and independence. As Benjamin Franklin (a London apprentice at this time) put it years later:

Having contracted with my subscribers to furnish them with what might be either useful or entertaining, I could not fill their pages with private altercation in which they had no concern, without doing them manifest injustice... In the conduct of my newspaper, I carefully excluded all libelling and personal abuse... Whenever I was solicited to insert anything of that kind, and the writer pleaded, as they generally did, the liberty of the press, and that a newspaper was like a stagecoach in which any who would pay had a right to a place, my answer was that I would print the piece separately if desired and the author might have as many copies as he pleased to distribute himself.

Franklin's *Autobiography* (written 1771–90, and published shortly after his death in 1793) is a useful, if somewhat coded, source for this period of British printing history. From the age of 18 until he was almost 21, Franklin lived and worked in London, passing along 'sleeping' Fleet Street every morning on his way from his lodgings in Craven Street, 'by Charing Cross', to his various printing jobs in Holborn and the St Paul's district. Unfortunately, his write-up of those days, done more than 50 years later, was imbued with revenge and can be very misleading. He never actually 'conducted' a newspaper in London, and to suggest 'honesty is the best policy' was simply to give good advice to any American arriving in London in 'dangerous' times. It did not reveal those occasions when he had found dishonesty to be the best policy. He was also much more self-indulgently worldly as well as rebellious than the youthful character he created for himself. He had been promised a 'gentlemanly' place in London at the King's Printing House. It proved to be an empty promise. He ended up 'working at press, as though I needed the exercise as an American, in Watt's great printing house near Lincoln's Inn Fields'. He felt humiliated and bore a grudge against his Anglo-American patron for the rest of his life.

Franklin arrived in London for the first time in December 1724, shortly after the trial of Nathaniel Mist, owner of *Mist's Weekly Journal*, had reached its 'crippling' conclusion. (He was sentenced to a year's imprisonment and fined £1,500, a colossal sum in those days, for publishing comments offensive to the government.) Franklin noted, with some satisfaction, that 'Mist's treasonable papers were being sold for half a guinea' as a consequence of his prosecution. He 'treasured this thought' for future reference. He also noted that Daniel Defoe, one of Mist's chief writers, 'was at pains to hide his connection'. He resolved to become 'an all-rounder in printing', to start his own newspaper, and to improve the working conditions of his fellow pressmen. He very soon proposed 'some reasonable alterations in their chapel laws, and carried them against all opposition'. He does not fully explain what this entailed, but it was clearly something more militant than simply 'giving up strong beer to stop muddling'.

My constant attendance [he concludes], I never making a St Monday, recommended me to the master, and my uncommon quickness at composing occasioned my being put upon all work of dispatch, which was generally better paid. So I went on very agreeably till the end [July 1726]. I cast types; I also engraved several things on occasion; I made the ink; I was a warehouseman and everything, and in short, quite a factotum.

Thomas Paine (1737–1809), radical Quaker writer and debater with a strong aversion to monarchy, became the toast of Fleet Street even before the French Revolution, following the publication of his rousing message to flagging Americans: 'These are the times that try mens' souls.' (Portrait by Auguste Millière)

Franklin returned to London in 1757 and again during the 1780s, by which time he had become famous as a publisher, inventor, educator, bon vivant and statesman. But he never lost his 'thoughts of making reprisals on my adversaries', and his eagerness to help Fleet Street dissidents, such as Tom Paine and William Duane, escape to America was known to everyone, including the authorities.

In the State Papers of 1721, there is a well-argued letter from an anonymous correspondent who suggests that it might be a good idea to produce a government newspaper to be sold at $\frac{1}{2}d$. to undercut all the rest. This would be a better way of dealing with the 'unruly' press than prosecuting printers and publishers: 'I will venture to affirm that there never was a Mist taken up or tryed but double the number of papers were sold upon it, besides the irritating of the people from the false notion of persecution.' The letter is marked approvingly, suggesting that the government had already begun to think along such lines, although it would never stoop to a halfpenny paper to carry official news! Bribery was much cheaper than prosecution, until it was discovered, when Walpole fell from power in 1742, that £50,077 18s. had been paid to authors and printers of various newspapers 'such as Free Britons, Daily Courants, Corn-Cutters' Journals, Gazetteers, and other political papers between 10 February 1731 and 10 February 1741'. Needless to say, this information was restricted to the Committee of Secrecy appointed to look into Walpole's affairs.

Much more threatening to investors in 'general' newspapers were the monthly literary magazines, which appeared in the 1730s. These may be seen as forerunners of the 'qualipops' or down-market 'qualities' (such as *The Guardian* and *The Observer*) revamped in the 1980s to broaden their appeal. They were immediately successful with the 'fashionable' reading public because they carried 'amusing' rather than 'overly respectful' speech reports based on the regular proceedings of Parliament.

As early as 1711, Abel Boyer (a Huguenot 'Whig' editor working for Tory proprietor Abel Roper, in a most independent manner) had produced a dull and very expensive *Political State of Great Britain* newsletter containing cautious accounts of speeches 'believed made' in the previous session. It was in open defiance of a parliamentary resolution (and the advice of Mr Roper). It also proved to be too far out of date to arouse much interest. Edward Cave, printer-proprietor of the new *Gentleman's Magazine*, was much more enterprising. He hired Dr Samuel Johnson, 'the best talker in Fleet Street', to report 'imaginatively' on the most topical debates, as though they had taken place in a Roman assembly, with speeches by Scipio Africanus, Tullius Cicero, and so on. It was a daring idea, being highly provocative as well as amusing, and it started a trend.

On 1 January 1731, the first number of the *Gentleman's Magazine*, printed by Nichols & Sons in Red Lion Court (169 Fleet Street), appeared in 'all the very best coffee-houses in London'. It was laid out like a book and began with a short table of contents, so that the reader could see at a glance what delights lay in store for him. These included 'A View of the Weekly Essays and Public Controversies', poetry, domestic occurrences, a paper on witchcraft, prices of goods and stocks, lists of bankrupts, sheriffs for the coming year, remarkable advertisements, foreign affairs, books and pamphlets just published, observations on gardening, and a list of fairs for the season. But the *pièce de résistance*, according to Boswell, was Johnson's elegant ridiculing of parliamentary non-oratory. 'If this is *not* what they said, it's what they should have said', was the 'insolent' idea behind the 'Controversies' series – and judging by the number of times Cave was able to persuade Johnson to repeat his brilliant opening performance, this seems to have been the general reaction.

Wisely, the government refrained from taking any immediate action. 'Leave him alone,' said Henry Pelham, 'he makes better speeches for us than we make ourselves' – which prompted several other magazines to come out in the same

SAMUEL JOHNSON
L.L.D.
CRITIC ESSAYIST PHILOLOGIST
BIOGRAPHER WIT POET MORALIST

vein. First it was the *London Magazine* (1732); then *The Inglenook* (1773), later *The Idler*, followed in due course by many others. With suitable modification of the contents from time to time (dictated by such things as the death of Cave in 1754 and the renewal of the parliamentary resolution), the *Gentleman's Magazine* managed to survive until 1907. But it very soon lost its concern to be sharp and topical when Johnson's parliamentary artistry went elsewhere in the 1750s.

Fleet Street was now 'much more welcoming to pen-pushers than to pressmen', according to young Henry Fielding. When he arrived for work there in 1727, he had, he says, 'no choice but to be a hackney writer or a hackney coachman'. Like Benjamin Franklin, he wanted desperately to become a printer, 'a trade that would support me forever, despite the slave-wages offered to apprentices'. Instead, he became a lawyer's scrivener or letter-writing clerk. While reading for the Bar, he nearly starved to death in a garret in Fetter Lane, and had no success at all with the new magazines. 'I offered them paragraphs to no avail. This article called Home News was the new common hunt.' Twenty years later, while rushing to the rescue of the Whig cause against the Jacobites in the first number of *The True Patriot* (5 November 1745), Fielding, the successful novelist and hack journalist, vented his spleen on contemporary newspapers:

> There is scarcely a syllable of TRUTH in any of them. If this be admitted to be a fault, it requires no other evidence than themselves and the perpetual contradictions which occur, not only on comparing one with another, but the same author with himself on different days. Second, there is no SENSE in them. Thirdly, there is in reality NOTHING in them at all. Such are the arrival of my Lord – with a great equipage; the marriage of Miss – of great beauty and merit; and the death of Mr – , who was never heard of in his life etc.

By mid-century, Fleet Street had become a tourist trap as well as the main distribution centre for most London newspapers. It was the central meeting-place for newsmen, providing the City with functional intelligence. It was also a gossip-factory, turning the winks and nods of taverners into 'news' about celebrities. But for most visitors, especially those from overseas, it was Johnson's London and a chance to see all the literary men of the period at their leisure. At the Fleet Ditch end, beyond the central conduit and water fountain near St Bride's, were 'many dubious lodging houses' carrying 'garish' signs and housing 'debtors, abortionists, prostitutes and ex-clergymen'. There were also 'skinners, dyers and numerous small tradesmen, ready to do anything for money'. Franklin, writing about his second stay in London in 1757, adds disapprovingly:

> The inhabitants of this disreputable part of London choose voluntarily to live much by candlelight and sleep by sunshine and yet often complain, a little absurdly, of the duty on candles and the high price of tallow.

Up near Temple Bar, opposite St Dunstan's, there was a very popular waxwork museum, 'the Tussaud collection of that day', run by 'the celebrated Mrs Salmon, who teaches the full art, and sells all sorts of moulds and glass eyes'. There was also a Royal Wigmaker, several tailors specializing in law robes, a 'statuary'

'Samuel Johnson L.L.D. ... Critic, essayist, philologist, biographer, wit, poet, novelist, dramatist, political writer, talker ... born 1709, died 1784. The gift and handiwork of Percy Fitzgerald F.S.A. 1910'. Standing outside his favourite church, St Clement Dane's, Dr Johnson is shown gazing paternally down the Fleet Street he loved so intemperately. (From *London's Immortals: The Complete Outdoor Commemorative Statues* by John Blackwood, Savoy Press)

41

called Rackstraw's Museum of Anatomy and Curiosities, John Murray's 'famous' bookshop, several taverns (i.e. coffee-houses) and four 'snuff boxes' or tobacconists. (In 1799, J. M. W. Turner exhibited his famous *Naumachia*, or Battle of the Nile canvas, 'in Silver Street, Bouverie Street and Fleet Street, receiving the applause of overflowing audiences'. This, we are told by T. C. Noble, 'was probably the last "raree-show" seen in the Street'.)

It is important to note, however, that there was not one composing room anywhere in 'the Street', until one was set up in the Temple in the last decade of the century. And even this operated 'more like a cookshop' for a whole host of short-lived, shoe-string newspapers compiled largely in taverns. Clearly, it could not begin to compare with the large, 100-men production centres operating in and around Little Britain. Nor would it be able to cope with the fine book printing, done mostly by guild printers in Paternoster Row. 'Ruffianism' had driven a lot of the 'gentlemanly' book business into the Strand and elsewhere. Tourism was said to be drawing the wrong sort of customer, even for John Murray who later moved to Albemarle Street, off Piccadilly. But Fleet Street, it was generally agreed, was 'the centre of the universe' for news. Its coffee-houses were 'exceptional' and catered for all classes and age-groups, from MPs and merchants to warehousemen and wharfmen. They also provided a 'clubland' as well as a 'press-room' for some of the best-informed men in Europe.

Voltaire, during his two years in London (following a short spell in the Bastille for being too witty about an aristocrat) says he spent much of his free time in Fleet Street. In his *Letters concerning the English Nation*, published in English in 1733, he tells how he would always try to meet his friend, Lord Bolingbroke, at 'the notorious Saracen's Head in Fleet Street'. He does not, of course, explain why. He also met Isaac Newton and John Locke, 'by pure chance', at a 'nearby coffee-house', after speculating in financial securities at the Royal Exchange.

'Come into the London Exchange', he enthuses Gallically, capturing the bon-homie of these two closely-related worlds like a true-born Londoner:

> It is a place more respectable than many a court. You will see assembled representatives of every nation for the benefit of mankind. Here the Jew, the Mohametan, and the Christian deal with one another as if they were of the same religion, and reserve the name 'infidel' for those who go bankrupt. Here the Presbyterian puts his trust in the Anabaptist, and the Anglican accepts the Quaker's promissory note. And all are content.

The Exchange also had room for anti-clerical libertine writers like John Wilkes and William Hone, Tom Paine and Benjamin Franklin. They, too, were men of the world who reserved the name 'infidel' for those who go bankrupt. They were prepared to use Fleet Street as a 'try-out' theatre for more widely saleable ideas. They also gambled with their lives like stock-jobbers in the cause of liberty and free enterprise. John Wilkes, the biggest gambler of them all, acquired an independent fortune through speculation and became a millionaire. His weekly journal, *The North Briton* (1762–3), brought him great influence in the City as well

as notoriety, and led directly to his being returned to Parliament as the 'popular member for Middlesex', after first becoming Lord Mayor.

On 3 February 1731 there appeared *The Daily Advertiser*, a single leaf only, intended 'to consist wholly of Advertisements, together with the Prices of Stocks, Course of Exchange, and names and descriptions of Persons becoming Bankrupts'. It was somewhat ahead of its time: a daily paper could not yet succeed on advertisements alone. It quickly became a standard newspaper of four pages, with a heavy emphasis on trade news. But the age of the 'Advertiser' had begun, with more and more papers adopting the word in their subtitle, and ever-increasing space being filled with advertisements concerning 'elixirs' or opium-based medicines, quack cures for venereal diseases and all sorts of 'illicit romance and seduction books'. At this point, newspaper advertising became a significant element in total revenue: in 1731, with a huge and expensive (country) circulation of some 12,000, *The Craftsman* (the first anti-government journal to be operated by a group of politicians) claimed that half of its paper and printing costs were 'regularly' covered by advertising.

Another major change initiated in Fleet Street at this time was the advent of shorthand. John Gurney, a clockmaker by trade, had spent much of his youth as a reporter in the Old Bailey trying desperately to provide the magistrates with a reliable record of the day's proceedings. Sometime in the 1750s, he managed to systematize his method of abbreviating words and phrases sufficiently to enable members of his family to take on similar work in other courts. Thus began a line of

'The Battle of Temple Bar', 22 March 1769, between supporters and opponents of Wilkes, took place when he petitioned to have his re-election to the Commons confirmed. Centre left is Nando's, the second coffee-house to be opened in London, which offered some sanctuary to the harassed envoys from the City while their coach was being searched.

A Champion of English Freedom

JOHN WILKES
1727-1797
MEMBER OF PARLIAMENT
LORD MAYOR

Gurneys who practised their eponymous system in Parliament itself for more than a century.

It was Gurney's system of 'brachygraphy' which the Dickens family learnt so profitably: John Dickens (father of Charles) and John Henry Barrow (Charles's brother-in-law), both worked very long hours for very good pay at the tedious business of producing verbatim reports about Parliament for newspapers. And when Charles Dickens refers, in a much-quoted passage from *David Copperfield*, to having 'tamed the savage stenographic system', he was alluding to Gurney's brachygraphy, the fifteenth edition of which came out in 1824. Dickens used it in the Law Courts and, after 1832, in the reporting of Parliament for the Whig paper, *The True Sun*. This, and the various other systems which culminated in the universally-accepted system perfected by Pitman in 1837, gave reporters a much-needed touch of authority. It was a step away from prostitution towards a kind of professionalism. It made them seem more like engineers and less like spies. It also separated the story-teller from the reporter.

Daniel Defoe, professional liar and journalist extraordinary, made no distinction between his creative spy-reports for the government and his amazing eye-witness accounts for the general public. They were simply assignments, writing jobs that came to him on impulse or on recommendation. They had nothing to do with objective reporting. He had no strong allegiance to anyone or anything outside Grub Street, not even to the truth. Defoe saw himself as a professional story-teller. Verisimilitude rather than truth was his stock-in-trade. It was better, in his view, to tell a good story, with an intriguing opening, an absorbing middle and a satisfying ending, than to confuse the customer with an assortment of unrelated facts in some tedious, over-long report. It was also advisable to take extra care to be accurate when using measurements or facts that could be easily verified (such as the width and number of steps to the main door of St Paul's).

On the other hand, William 'Memory' Woodfall, editor, printer and sole 'staffer' of the popular *Morning Chronicle*, was a different kind of professional, more of a civil servant than a civil libertarian. He would not permit anything to be published in his paper that was not the literal truth. He had a news monopoly to protect, parliamentary debates, and he was not going to offend MPs by abusing his special place in the Visitors' Gallery. Remarkably, he managed to cover a whole day's proceedings in the House of Commons by himself, using only his memory (note-taking was not allowed) as a recording device. Almost everything that happened there (he was told by the Sergeant-at-Arms), even the tomfoolery, was covered by privilege and must be treated with great respect if criminal libel was to be avoided. Whatever he decided to release from his memory-bank and relate in print to a marvelling audience must have been uttered in the House and be clearly attributed to some Member. It was enough to deter the Recording Angel! Even so, many readers preferred Woodfall's neat paraphrases to the new, over-long, verbatim shorthand reports.

Samuel Johnson's so-called parliamentary reports were, on his own admission,

William 'Memory' Woodfall (1746–1803), known as 'the father of modern reporting'. Founder editor (in 1769) of the *Morning Chronicle* and pioneer of Parliamentary reporting, Woodfall generally managed to 'cover' a whole day's proceedings by himself, using only his memory as a recording device – note-taking was not allowed.

Opposite This aggressive-looking statue of John Wilkes in Fetter Lane, just off Fleet Street, was 'erected by admirers' led by Dr James Cope (on the left), who unveiled it in 1988. On the right is James Butler, RA, the sculptor. The image represents Wilkes delivering his famous speech as MP in 1776, introducing a Bill 'for the Just and Equal Representation of the People of England in Parliament'.

Dr Samuel Johnson (1709–84), lexicographer, and James Boswell (1740–95), his Scottish biographer, dined together frequently in the Mitre Tavern, Fleet Street, where Johnson was renowned for his conversation and Boswell for his womanizing.

largely imaginative concoctions. They were written 'with a feeling of impatience', to instruct the governors rather than the governed, according to Boswell. The idea, presumably, was 'to turn dross into gold'. But Johnson was not overly pleased with his journalistic success: he seemed to be fooling too many people too much of the time. 'Irony has no place in a newspaper', he concluded, and he quickly retreated from 'working' journalism into his *Dictionary* and other literary pursuits.

Sir John Hawkins relates how, when Johnson was dining with close friends at the old Mitre Tavern in Fleet Street, conversation turned on a speech by Pitt the Elder. 'Many of the company remembered the debate,' we are told,

and many passages were cited from the speech, with the approbation and applause of all present. During the ardour of the conversation, Johnson remained silent. When the warmth of praise subsided, he opened his mouth with these words: 'That speech I wrote in a garret in Exeter Street.' The company was struck with astonishment... Dr Francis asked how that speech could be written by him. 'Sir,' said Dr Johnson, 'I wrote it in Exeter Street. I never was in the gallery of the House of Commons but once. Cave had an interest with Bellamy, the doorkeeper. He and the

46

persons under him got admittance. They brought away the subject of discussion, the names of the speakers, the side they took, and the order in which they rose, together with notes of the various arguments adduced in the course of the debate. The whole was afterwards communicated to me, and I composed the speeches in the form they now have in *Parliamentary Debates*, for the speeches of that period [1740–3] are all printed from Cave's Magazine.'

To this discovery Dr Francis made answer: 'Then, sir, you have exceeded Demosthenes himself!' The rest of the company were lavish in their compliments to Johnson. One in particular praised his impartiality, observing that he had dealt out reason and eloquence with an equal hand to both parties.

'That is not quite true, sir,' said Johnson: 'I saved appearances well enough, but I took good care that the Whig dogs should not have the best of it.'

18 Red Lion Court was an early centre of printing during the 1760s, when John Nichols produced the *Gentleman's Magazine*. Even in 1969, when this photo was taken, its outer wall was still carrying the ornate emblem of Abraham Valpy, a book printer of the 1820s.

In other words, Johnson was a party hack for several years and hated himself for it. He was eventually relieved of the drudgery by the bestowal of a Crown pension of £300 a year in 1762. From then on, he was in the 'celebrity' business. The Fleet Street Literary Club, of which he was a founder member (1764), was the chief place where his genius shone amid a galaxy of other talent subsidized by the book trade. He 'never moved a biscuit toss from his beloved Fleet Street', according to John Gore, and died peacefully in his bed at 8 Bolt Court in 1784. (Gore gives his 'Odyssey' as follows: Strand, Boswell Court, 1738; Holborn, Fetter Lane, Holborn again; Gough Square, 1749–50; Staple Inn, Gray's Inn, 1 Inner Temple Lane – the present site of Johnson's Buildings – 7 Johnson's Court and, finally, 8 Bolt Court.)

In the 1770s, as it became easier for reporters with shorthand to gain and retain admission to the two Houses of Parliament, Opposition members began addressing their speeches direct to the pressmen in the Visitors' Gallery. They yearned to be included 'in the first draft of history' and felt they would be bound to get a better showing than the government because what they had to say was much closer to what those outside the House wished to hear. However, in striving to make politics 'interesting' for the first time, they also managed to play right into the hands of an information-starved Fleet Street whose decision to take up a political stance was dictated largely by profit.

In 1773, William 'Memory' Woodfall was publicly accused of taking £400 per annum from Fox and Sheridan to ensure they were reported at greater length than Pitt and Dundas. He denied taking money, claiming he was merely acceding to 'public interest'. But when his patrons dismissed the charge as 'electioneering', the worst conclusion was drawn and the practice became general throughout Fleet Street. Woodfall was eventually forced out of business, but not by the authorities, who ruled by bribery. He was defeated by age and by James Perry (1756–1821), editor of *The London Gazetteer*, who had perfected a new system of reporting debates: he employed young 'and impecunious' barristers to take shorthand notes in relays, half-an-hour at a time. Woodfall's paper, 'a one-man band for years', collapsed when he collapsed. Perry took it over, turning the *Morning Chronicle* into an impressive instrument which far outstripped *The Times* in its early years, and survived until a bad investment in 1882.

Once free of *The London Gazetteer*, a 'ministerial' paper heavily subsidized by the government, Perry steadfastly refused to take insertion and correction fees from anyone: nor would he accept free theatre tickets in exchange for printing puffs. 'It will be essentially better', he wrote to one theatre manager, 'for both of us to put an end to this pitiful arrangement, and resolve in future to pay for admission to each other's premises.' He also hired writers of distinction and critical awareness, 'who would not be tempted by publishers' bribes'. These included R. B. Sheridan, Sir James Mackintosh, William Hazlitt on theatre, and Tom Moore on gossip. It was Perry, therefore, and not Thomas Barnes (Hazlitt's counterpart on *The Times*, until Barnes became editor in 1817) who pioneered the way to modern editorship and freedom from book publishers.

Perry, more than anyone, was able to professionalize the management function of newspaper editing as much as the production function. He did this by 'massing' his advertisements, collecting so much that he was often 'hard-pressed to find room for all his Whig propaganda'. He had bought the paper partly with his own money, 'entirely with the sums raised by his personal efforts from private friends'. Despite his strong Whiggish inclinations, he got no help whatsoever from the Whig leader, Charles James Fox, who boasted that when abroad on holiday he only opened a daily paper to see the racecourse odds.

The sole grandee from whom Perry received both insider information and financial encouragement was the Duke of Norfolk. He presented the *Morning Chronicle* with a set of palatial offices in one of the unlet houses (No. 332) on his Strand property. He also offered to advise Perry on what was really going on behind the scenes. This might have helped him to solve the whole riddle out of which the modern newspaper was born, namely, how to acquire information regarding the control of society while remaining separate from the government. But it seems Perry did not make much use of this 'Deep Throat' opportunity. According to T. H. S. Escott, 'he left the graver matters to a Mr. Gray, an assistant master at Charterhouse School, who had just come into a legacy'.

Gray was 'a proud man', who heartily disliked the Duke of Norfolk. He was also, says Escott, 'a man of first-rate intellectual power who, had his life been spared longer, would have taken higher and better known rank among the personal forces that created and controlled the English newspaper of the eighteenth and nineteenth centuries'. Little more is known about this intriguing Mr Gray (not even his initials) except that, in return for his investment of £500, he became assistant editor, 'lived over the shop' and, at all critical times, 'was the one who pulled the labouring oar'. For example, it was Gray who posted a man to Paris, 'out of his own pocket', to monitor the events in depth after the Revolution broke out in 1789.

As for Perry, Escott goes on to say:

> the great qualities which had raised him to a position more commanding, perhaps, than had been won by any of his predecessors or contemporaries, went together with an inordinate fondness, which he never outgrew, for seeing himself in print. His personal vanity was never more gra-

tified than when the public persisted in attributing to his inspiration, if not handiwork, all that was freshest, brightest or best in any particularly striking issue.

In other words, Perry was a belletrist rather than a hard-nosed journalist; a managing rather than a tough, technocrat editor; an exhibitionist rather than a sensationalist.

Daniel Stuart, editor of the *Morning Post*, was the complete opposite. His Perthshire brothers were already well started in a London printing business when he joined them in Catherine Street, opposite Somerset House, in 1778. Five years later, he had turned the *Post* from a weak Whig paper into a strong Tory 'rag' by means of 'blackmail, extortion, advertising and a large Government subsidy'. His writers included Charles Lamb, Leigh Hunt, Coleridge; and Southey, who surprised nobody when he suddenly handed over his literary criticism to William Wordsworth, saying newspaper men were pestilent nuisances who would destroy the Constitution if they were not first exterminated themselves.

Stuart's primary concern was to build up the advertisement side of his business so that he could become independent of government control. He succeeded better than most. 'One day, an official came to me with a message of thanks from the prime minister, Mr. Addington, offering me anything I wished. I declined the offer', says Stuart. From that point on, the commercial situation allowed independence if it were desired. As early as 1784, the *Morning Post* made a profit of £1,500.

James Perry (1756–1821), 'the King of London journalism', owner-editor of the *Morning Chronicle* and humane liberal, 'created the profession of journalism' (according to press historian Charles Pebody) by hiring writers proud enough to resist the temptation of publishers' bribes as well as pressures from the Home Office.

Founder of a dynasty: John Walter I, retired coal merchant, invented the Logographic Press and also in 1785 launched *The Daily Universal Register*, which three years later became *The Times*.

Throughout the nineties, it was making between £40 and £50 a day from closely packed advertisements, despite the tax having been raised to 3s. in 1789. The income from more dubious sources can only be guessed at, but it was considerable. It is also known that, in 1790, his subsidy from the government was £300. He bought the *Post* for £600 in 1783 and sold it for £25,000, just after Lamb had left him to work in 'more radical journalism' in 1795.

It was a different story over at *The Times*'s office in Printing House Square, which was rather prettily situated next door to the London home of the Walter family. In its early years, *The Times* was little more than a business information sheet, the lesser offshoot of a somewhat eccentric printing business started by a failed coal merchant. By 1795, John Walter I had grown tired of the enterprise and handed over, first to his eldest son, William, who, like James Perry, had more literary taste than journalistic flair, and then, in 1803, to his second son, John, who quickly made the paper profitable but fractured his relations both with his father and the government.

In 1805, *The Times* under John Walter II attacked Henry Dundas, Lord Melville, First Lord of the Admiralty and Pitt's closest colleague, accusing him of misappropriation of Admiralty funds. Although Melville was acquitted at the subsequent trial, Pitt decided to teach the Walter family a lesson. The licence granted to John Walter I to print Customs and other government notices was revoked, and orders were issued to confiscate all overseas dispatches received in the name of *The Times* at Gravesend.

John Walter II's response was to defy the government and to organize a system of dispatch running which could not be inspected and confiscated by naval officials. A cutter was chartered to run the blockade (it being wartime) and collect French newspapers from local fishermen. Parcels of letters were carried to the south coast by smugglers and thence by special courier to Printing House Square. This foreign news was published several days before the government could release similar information to other London newspapers. Walter's success is indicated by the fact that *The Times* was able to publish the first news of the Battle of Trafalgar. On 6 November 1806, Plumer Ward wrote to Lord Lowther:

> I am almost ashamed to send your Lordship a newspaper as the latest news from the Continent, but I assure you *The Times* publishes, seemingly from authority, more than can have been officially received, from the state of the packet boats and the winds.

A letter to John Walter II from the Foreign Office, dated 18 September 1813[7] states:

> Mr Hamilton presents his compliments to Mr Walter, and is directed by Lord Castlereagh to request that he will have the goodness to tell him if he has received any Intelligence of the reported defeat of the French near Dresden, which is now in circulation.

This was more than sweet revenge: it was independent power based on a news service second to none. *The Times* was already on its way to establishing its extraordinary dominance in the years to come. By 1823, William Hazlitt, an ex-employee of the paper, could write in *The Edinburgh Review* that *The Times* was:

> the greatest engine of temporary opinion in the world.... It is the witness of the British metropolis; the mouthpiece, oracle and echo of the Stock Exchange, the origin of the mercantile interest.... It takes up no falling causes; fights no uphill battle; advocates no great principle... It is ever stronger upon the stronger side.

Hazlitt, with French-style 'fraternité' in mind, clearly disapproved of *The Times*'s attitude towards its readers. It was élitist rather than democratic: business-oriented rather than people-oriented. He was disgusted that, in such stirring times, it should be content merely to marshal its readers together for special consideration as businessmen, rather than goad them into a republican revolution in which everybody might benefit. Business forces had indeed triumphed over the feudal forces of repression. They had even opened up the exciting possibility of

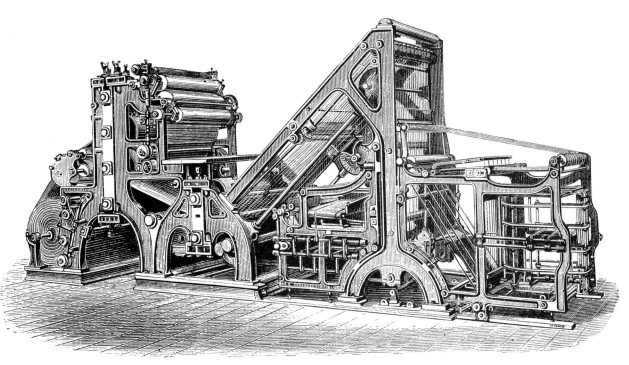

This privately developed Walter Press was based on the first rotary press, produced by Robert Hoe in New York in 1846.

actually sharing political power with the property-owning 'Establishment', to use the famous word of his friend, Cobbett. But they had not, in his view, addressed themselves to the important humanitarian questions for Britain raised by the French Revolution.

> Twenty-six millions of our fellow creatures bursting their chains and throwing off, almost in an instant, the degrading yoke of slavery – is a scene so new, interesting and sublime that the heart which cannot participate in the triumph must have been vitiated by illiberal politics or be naturally depraved.

Hazlitt was only ten years old when the French Revolution erupted in May 1789. Born in Maidstone, Kent, the son of a Unitarian minister, he had just returned to London from America, which his father had found to be 'seriously wanting as regards personal liberty'. He held all his life to the conviction that the French Revolution was the dawn of a new era, even when it eventually fell far short of expectations. Not even Tom Paine's 'clarion call for freedom' was thought to be 'fanatical' enough for what Hazlitt had in mind for Britain. As he told his friend Charles Lamb, he 'had to wait for William Cobbett to return from America for that'. For Charles James Fox, leader of the official Opposition, the French Revolution was 'the greatest event that ever happened in the history of the world'; for Josiah Wedgwood, 'it threw the political world off its hinges'; and 'For people of all times of life everywhere [according to Leigh Hunt], a thousand new channels of thought and interest have been opened up.'

Its effect on British Radicalism, with all its abstract theories about natural rights and the equality of men, was similar to that of the Russian Revolution of 1917 on Communism. Here, at last, was a country actually daring to turn theory

into hard political reality. Suddenly, the theories were not as abstract and idealistic as their opponents' thoughts. And, for the first time since John Wilkes and his *North Briton*, Fleet Street energies were turned towards political sensationalism and radical 'disclosures', for purely ideological reasons. It all began with a sermon, delivered to a packed audience of shopkeepers, artisans and mechanics gathered in John Wesley's London headquarters, the Moravian Chapel in Fetter Lane, in November 1789. The speaker was Dr Richard Price (1723–91), the leading dissenting minister in London, and his message, beginning: 'The times are auspicious. Tremble all ye oppressors of the world', was (according to Sampson Perry, a radical editor) 'like a thunder-clap of freedom' after a long, hot summer of frustration. 'Let us be thankful', said Price, 'for a diffusion of knowledge which has undermined superstition and error.'

Edmund Burke's famous response to this sermon, *Reflections on the Revolution*

William Hazlitt (1778–1830), artist, essayist and freelance journalist, went to Printing House Square as drama critic in 1817, but stayed only six months. Thereupon *The Times* (28 August 1823) referred to him as 'a discarded servant' who should not be allowed to 'bespatter and scandalize his employer'.

53

in France, was published in Fleet Street early in 1790, sparking off what has since been termed 'A Revolution by Correspondence'. His message was equally clear. English radicals should not copy their French counterparts. The aristocratic and hierarchical English past and present must and will be defended from its enemies. At a time when the public and private language of most people outside Parliament (with the notable exception of the business press) was full of unrestrained welcome for 'the wonderful revolution', this was a deliberately provocative call for reaction from one of the foremost political thinkers in England. It brought him a civil list pension of £1,200 a year, granted in 1795.

The first to reply to Burke was James Mackintosh, chief leader writer on the *Morning Chronicle*. His *Vindiciae Gallicae* came out in January 1791, advocating the principles of freedom and humanity. It was aimed at young Whig lawyers like himself and was not written in anything that could be called a popular style. Even so, according to Richard Cobden, 'it was written with a far closer logic and in a style scarcely less attractive than that of his great opponent'. William Godwin (1756–1836) rose next to the occasion, with his philosophical *Inquiry concerning Political Justice*, a considerable treatise written in what Shelley described as 'mandarin language'. He was followed by Mary Wollstonecraft (1759–97) with her *A Vindication of the Rights of Man* (1790) and *A Vindication of the Rights of Woman* (1792).

But none of the 38 replies noted by Conor Cruise O'Brien would be so powerful and so popular as Thomas Paine's *The Rights of Man*, the first part of which appeared in February 1791. It caused a sensation, not simply because it was seditious but because it was so confident. He offered an ingratiating, ruminative, readable document which talked about democracy democratically. He supplied facts and figures to back up his argument (Part II was even better in this respect) and, because these were not generally known, managed to give the impression that revolution had already begun in Britain itself.

Paine had been trying desperately to finish his work before the opening of Parliament in February 1791. He succeeded. But the printer to whom he gave the work, a man named Johnson, became frightened because so many of the sentiments expressed 'were so unbuttoned'. Johnson gave up the enterprise after printing only a handful of copies (most of which were sold in New York). Paine was forced to seek another printer, thus missing his deadline. J. S. Jordan, whose printshop had just opened at 166 Fleet Street, agreed to take the work, providing one sentence – 'Everything in the English government appears to me the reverse of what it ought to be, and of what it is said to be' – was taken out. Reluctantly, Paine agreed. He left the publication in the hands of his friends, William Godwin and playwright Thomas Holcroft, departing for France just prior to the first uninterrupted publication of Part I of *The Rights of Man* on 13 March 1791.

It cost 3*s*. but, even so, managed to outsell Burke's pamphlet in a very few weeks. The first printing of 10,000 copies sold out overnight and thereafter Jordan kept his presses running day and night in an attempt to meet the demand. Paine

Thomas Paine, somewhat belatedly adopted as a 'Prominent American' for his stirring, upbeat messages to American revolutionaries in 1776: a 1968 reissue by the US Mail.

was urged to bring out a cheaper edition, and Part II, which appeared in February 1792, was issued not only as a 3s. pamphlet but also in a 6d. edition. Within a month, 32,000 were sold, and the cheap edition continued to sell strongly for years, totalling at least two million copies in Great Britain, the USA and France. Paine refused to accept any payment for what he regarded as 'a simple necessity to tell the truth'. He insisted that all of the proceeds be paid to the Society for Constitutional Information (founded in 1780 by Major John Cartwright), which acquired large sums as a result.

Paine's message that 'all men are born equal and with equal natural right', had a galvanizing effect on the reform movement. It seemed to be directing them to turn sensationalism into a political tool. His work also demonstrated the political effectiveness of well-researched, investigative journalism, hitherto a low form of blackmail and character assassination. Even respectable, middle-class journalists like Charles Lamb felt 'joyously rebellious' after reading it; 'our occupation

Yours ratherish unwell

Chs Lamb

Charles Lamb (1775–1834), essayist, was born in the Temple, where his father was clerk to a wealthy Bencher. At Christ's Hospital, 1782–9, he met Leigh Hunt and Thomas Barnes, who later introduced him to Hazlitt; they all subsequently wrote for *The Examiner*. Caricature by David Maclise in Fraser's Magazine, 1835.

now,' he said later, 'was to write treason.' A myriad of radical publications, such as *Hog's Wash* (1793) and *The Telegraph* (1794), appeared almost overnight, many part-financed by Paine's earnings, all produced in the Fleet Street district. Militant printers and journeymen, newly arrived from high-rent areas around Aldgate and Paternoster Row, were said to be more afraid of mechanization than of investigation by 'that English Robespierre', William Pitt.

The government had lost heavily in the courts, due mainly to Fox's Libel Act of 1792, which empowered the jury instead of the judge to determine the criminality of a libel. Thomas Hardy, Horne Tooke and John Thelwall (close friends of the outlawed Tom Paine) had been acquitted of 'a traitorous and detestable conspiracy to supersede the House of Commons in its representative capacity'. All those arrested and held under the suspension of the Habeas Corpus Act had been released. 'Had these trials been otherwise decided,' wrote Major Cartwright years later, 'our history would have been written in innocent blood.' In his essay, 'Newspapers Thirty-Five Years Ago', published in 1831, Lamb recalls how he was 'suddenly and excitingly thrust into the radical struggle at this time'. Transferred from the offices of the 'respectable' *Morning Post* (situated 'awkwardly' opposite the Stamp Office in Somerset House) to the 'den' of the *Albion* newspaper, 'late Rackstrow's Museum in radical Fleet Street', Lamb enthuses:

What a transition that was... from the centre of loyalty and fashion to a focus of vulgarity and sedition! Here, in murky closet, sat the redoubted John Fenwick, resolutely determined upon pulling down the government in the first instance, and making both our fortunes by way of corollary.

It was his special job, Lamb says, 'to gently insinuate, rather than recommend, possible abdications. Blocks, axes, Whitehall tribunals etc. were covered with flowers of so cunning a periphrasis... that the keen eye of an Attorney General was insufficient to detect the lurking snake among them.'

Not all Fleet Street publications were quite so cautious, however, and it was into this highly-charged, rebellious atmosphere that William Duane, one-time parliamentary reporter for the *General Advertiser*, re-entered Fleet Street from India in 1795, to take over the editorship of *The Telegraph*, a Jacobin weekly which, according to a Home Office agent, 'generally had priority of intelligence over Ministerial prints'.

Duane was born in 1760 in colonial America (near Lake Champlain, New York), returning with his mother to her native Dublin in 1771. He was apprenticed to a Dublin printer at the age of 14; worked as a journalist in Dublin until he was 22; then moved to London in 1782 to work for the *General Advertiser*, until he was offered the editorship of a newspaper in Calcutta in 1786. He returned to London, 'penniless', in 1795, to find Fleet Street 'a most turbulent place', the epicentre of popular protest against 'the corrupt boroughmongering system'. He immediately joined the London Corresponding Society (LCS), founded by Thomas Hardy in Essex Street in 1792, and invited members to make use of his editorial office as a meeting room. For this, and 'other services to the radical cause', Duane was unanimously elected to chair the Society's second mass rally for reform, to be held in the Copenhagen Fields on 12 November, 1795.

At this point, there was a sharp change in the government's attitude towards political protest. Stone-throwings at George III while he was travelling to Westminster, together with other physical attacks on ministers following the first mass open-air meeting organized by the LCS, produced overt, punitive measures for the first time. On 4 November 1795, a royal proclamation exhorted magistrates 'to discourage, prevent and suppress all seditious and unlawful assemblies', and with astonishing rapidity, two bills were drawn up and presented to Parliament. The first, introduced on 6 November, extended the law relating to treason, making all actions against the person of George III, or his heirs, capital offences. Speech or writing offences inciting hatred were also made liable to a sentence of transportation to Australia for up to seven years. The other bill, introduced on 10 November 1795, restricted public meetings to less than 50 persons unless a magistrate was notified well in advance – which meant, among other things, that Duane could be charged with running 'a disorderly house'.

The bills drew loud protests from almost everybody, including moderate reformers like James Mackintosh, who abandoned journalism at this point to become a brilliant libel defence lawyer. Duane merely insisted, for all to take note, that the second planned meeting would proceed regardless. Incredibly, nearly 400,000 people are said to have attended this meeting, but we only have Duane's word for this. There is, however, no doubt that Duane signed the resolutions of the meeting, later published, stating that the people were 'on the verge of desperation' over the extinction of their remaining liberties. Duane was quick to point out (as have historians since) that the Acts would be the most crucial elements in the destruction of the popular radical movement that had begun in 1792. He was right. There was a warrant out for his arrest even before he had returned home from the meeting. He went into hiding, along with many others, and left for America soon after the bills received the royal assent on 18 December 1795.

Duane's arrival in Philadelphia in March 1796, along with several other Fleet Street refugees, could not have been better timed. It coincided with the rise of the democratic Jeffersonian party in that first capital of the young American republic. Thomas Jefferson was in dire need of experienced journalistic talent to respond in kind to the 'Billingsgate' (as he termed it), 'spewed out' by William Cobbett (writing under the name of Peter Porcupine) on behalf of the reactionary Federal press. Duane (armed with letters of introduction from Benjamin Frank-

Publisher Richard Carlile's 'free-thinking' ideas and Paineite writing, in a succession of illegally unstamped publications, led him into prison several times. His home and publishing office, at 62 Fleet Street, was known as 'The Temple of Reason' and was a principal centre of radical protest. This painting of Carlile was bequeathed by Chartist lecturer and disciple, G. J. Holyoake.

lin) was given a job as chief assistant to Benjamin Franklin Bache, ailing owner of the *Philadelphia General Advertiser and Aurora*. In December 1798, barely a month after he had taken over both the printing business and the editorship, Duane declared his intention of 'democratizing' the American press. Thus began a most abusive press 'war' ('The Dark Ages in American Journalism', according to Emery in 1978), which ended in victory at the polls for the Jeffersonians and defeat for the Federalists led by President John Adams.

Cobbett was forced to abandon what he confessed was 'an unequal struggle', returning to London in 1800 to start a completely new life. He could not deny the truth of Duane's findings: certain British diplomats had indeed been 'actively interfering with democracy at all levels of American government'. Duane's evidence (supplied to him by Jefferson) was incontrovertible: the British Treasury had spent $800,000 (£170,000) during 1798, trying to influence American policy towards France as well as American public opinion. The money had been distributed, Duane said, mainly in the form of newspaper subsidies. Cobbett denied being one of the recipients of such money. He admitted that he hated France, but insisted that he hated corruption even more. Duane simply repeated his charges: Cobbett, he said, was the 'shameless organizer of a witch-hunt' against certain British political exiles like himself. 'These are facts,' Duane concluded, 'which no perfidious artifice can evade, nor impudence deny... The people must endeavour to identify as well as they can the channels through which this corruption from Britain has circulated.'

Cobbett was greatly confused by the whole episode and remained in this condition for many months after his return to England. Left to himself and his prejudices, he was inclined to link Duane (and 'that drunkard, Tom Paine') with the French Terror in Paris rather than with the Pitt Terror in London. Not until he arrived in Fleet Street was he able to recognize Duane for what he most probably was, a victim rather than a practitioner of terror, interested only in 'democratizing' the American press.

Jefferson's encouragement of 'Jacobin journalism' had surprised everyone: even Duane thought he had made a friend for life. It had also helped the cause of democracy in Europe. It was 'a consolation' to Richard Carlile, and other Jacobin publishers such as W. T. Sherwin, during the darkest hours of the Pitt repression in London. Cobbett was as disgusted as anyone, therefore, when the news came that, 'for the sake of peace and party unity', Jefferson had been persuaded to drop Duane from his payroll soon after becoming the third President of the United States on 17 February 1801. By this time, Cobbett had been converted to radicalism, believing like Duane that journalists everywhere had 'an inalienable right' to shape the fate of a nation. He also believed that there would have been no Jeffersonian revolution in American politics if there had not been so many so-called 'foreign liars' on hand, 'fugitive felons from Fleet Street' according to ex-President Adams, anxious to spread the Jacobin word of 'popular democracy' among American newspaper readers.

3 'A Focus of Vulgarity and Sedition'

(Charles Lamb, 1831)

The French Revolution, which erupted in 1789, brought a new sense of common purpose into Fleet Street, changing it from a centre of limited loyalty and literary fashion into 'a focus of vulgarity and sedition'. Editorials recommending possible abdications 'were covered with flowers of so cunning a periphrasis… that the keen eye of an Attorney General was insufficient to detect the lurking snake among them'. Militant printers and journeymen, newly arrived from high-rent districts elsewhere, together with radical journalists like William Hazlitt and William Cobbett, were determined to show the world that they were much more afraid of losing their jobs through industrialization than of investigation by 'that English Robespierre, William Pitt'.

Right   Theodore Edward Hook, 'Theodore Flash', launched the original *John Bull* as a Sunday paper from 11 Johnson's Court in 1820, and continued it ('scandalous' to some, 'patriotic' to others) until his death 21 years later. (From *Old Fleet Street*, in the *London Recollected* series by G. W. Thornbury, reprinted by The Village Press)

Opposite Top Left   This likeness of George Cruikshank, caught by his fellow artist Daniel Maclise, appeared in *Fraser's Magazine*, 1833. Cruikshank, a prolific caricaturist on political and social themes, is buried in the crypt of St Paul's Cathedral, his tomb bearing the inscription 'in memory of his Genius and his Art'.

Top Right Crane Court housed the first tiny editorial offices of two famous publications: *Punch*, founded in 1841 at No. 9, and *The Illustrated London News*, founded in 1842 at No. 10. (From *Old Fleet Street*, in the *London Recollected* series by G. W. Thornbury, reprinted by The Village Press)

Right Herbert Ingram was the founder of a remarkable journalistic dynasty. In 1842 he launched *The Illustrated London News* and the publishing offices at 195–198 Strand (later named Ingram House) came to bear a plaque commemorating 'the world's first illustrated newspaper'. His son was knighted as Sir William, and his grandson (editor for 63 years) became Sir Bruce.

As a piece of furniture the 'PUNCH table is not of much account, but its associations make it special. It appeared shortly after 'PUNCH was started in 1841, and became established as the focal point of a literary and artistic legend. From its initiation — as a weekly dinner meeting between proprietors and staff — to the present, it has been the occasion for wit to strike sparks from wit, to broaden 'PUNCH's view of the world, to keep the Editor in touch with his staff, and through them, the public. More recently it has become the custom to invite distinguished guests to take part. Since the beginning, the staff have carved their initials on the Table, but only six 'Strangers' have been invited to become Table members. The initials of five are carved on the Table: H.R.H. Prince Philip, H.R.H. Prince Charles, H.R.H. Princess Anne, H.R.H. Princess Margaret and James Thurber. Mark Twain declined to carve saying that two-thirds of Thackeray's would suffice for him.

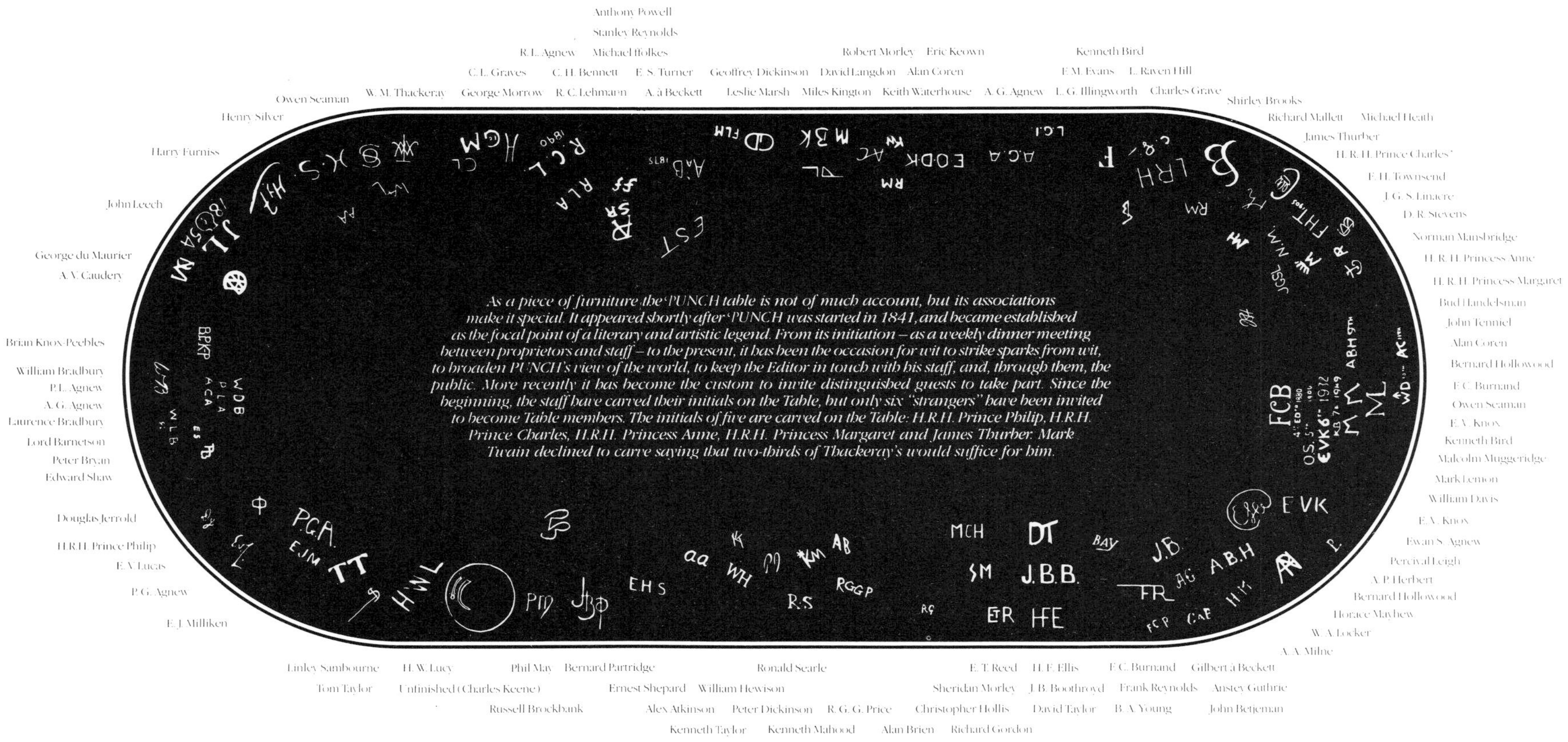

Anthony Powell
Stanley Reynolds
R. L. Agnew   Michael Ffolkes
C. L. Graves   C. H. Bennett   E. S. Turner   Geoffrey Dickinson   David Langdon   Alan Coren
W. M. Thackeray   George Morrow   R. C. Lehmann   A. J. Beckett   Leslie Marsh   Miles Kington   Keith Waterhouse   A. G. Agnew   L. G. Illingworth   Charles Grave   Shirley Brooks
Robert Morley   Eric Keown
Kenneth Bird
E. V. Evans   L. Raven Hill

Richard Mallett   Michael Heath
James Thurber
H. R. H. Prince Charles
E. H. Townsend
J. G. S. Izzard
D. R. Stevens
Norman Mansbridge
H. R. H. Princess Anne
H. R. H. Princess Margaret
Basil Hunderleman
John Tenniel
Alan Coren
Bernard Hollowood
F. C. Burnand
Owen Seaman
E. V. Knox
Kenneth Bird
Malcolm Muggeridge
Mark Lemon
William Davis
E. V. Knox
Evans Agnew
Patrick Cleugh
A. P. Herbert
Bernard Hollowood
Horace Mayhew
W. A. Hooker
A. A. Milne

Henri Silver
John Leech
George du Maurier
A. A. Cauden
Brian Knox Peebles
William Bradbury
P. L. Agnew
A. G. Agnew
Laurence Bradbury
Lord Burnerson
Peter Brun
Edward Sloan
Douglas Jerrold
H. R. H. Prince Philip
E. V. Lucas
P. G. Agnew
E. J. Milliken

Linley Sambourne
Tom Taylor
Russell Brockbank

H. W. Lucy   Phil May   Bernard Partridge   Ronald Searle
Unfinished Charles Keene
Alex Atkinson   Peter Dickinson   R. G. G. Price   Christopher Hollis   Sheridan Morley   E. T. Reed   H. F. Ellis   F. C. Burnand   Gilbert à Beckett
Kenneth Taylor   Kenneth Mahood   Alan Brien   Richard Gordon   Ernest Shepard   William Hewison   David Taylor   Frank Reynolds   Anstey Guthrie   B. A. Young   John Betjeman

Above The scene outside 198 Strand in 1851 when a special edition of *The Illustrated London News* came off the press.

Above Delivery of *The Illustrated London News* to Somerset House for stamping. This scene, in September 1852, took place three years before the newspaper stamp duties were repealed.

Opposite The Punch Table, still preserved in the new offices on the South Bank. It became a tradition for a working dinner (or luncheon) to be held for proprietors and senior staff, with distinguished guests occasionally invited to carve their initials on the table – known colloquially (but incorrectly) as 'The Mahogany Tree' – alongside those of their hosts.

Above Newsboys: an *Illustrated London News* artist, R. Ponsonby Staples, gives a graphic impression of *The Daily Chronicle* going on sale.

Opposite Top Henry Reeve (1813–95) was little known to the public until he became editor of *The Edinburgh Review*, but for 15 years in the mid-nineteenth century he was the 'thundering' anonymous voice of *The Times* in its foreign leaders.

Right The American-designed but British-built Hoe revolving-type press with sheet feed, as installed at *The Times* in 1857 by John Walter III.

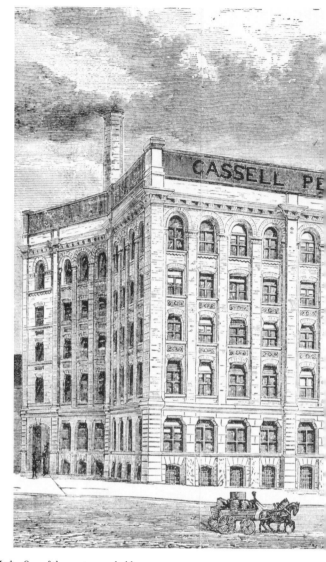

Left One of the most remarkable memorials in the City of London is that to Paul Julius Reuter, news agency promoter, outside the Royal Exchange. He founded his London office, and future international headquarters nearby, in October 1851.

Above Cassell, Petter & Galpin,
the publishers (and then printers
also), opened their massive La
Belle Sauvage works in Fleet
Lane, east of Ludgate Circus, in
1875. They had already launched
The Echo, an evening paper with
the highest circulation of its time.

Right Another champion of
popular education was the printer
and publisher Charles Knight. His
Fleet Street-based Society for the
Diffusion of Useful Knowledge
produced *The Penny Magazine*
and *The Penny Cyclopaedia*.

67

4 Personal Forces

If William Cobbett had fought, almost to the water's edge, against being forced to leave the United States, this was not simply because he had just lost a 'ridiculous' libel action. It was not even because he was doing so well in business with his two 'London Books' shops, one in Philadelphia, the other in New York. It was because he could not bring himself to admit that he might have been wrong. His famous patriotism, inflamed by years of argument with American Anglophobes, had produced in his mind an exile's England that bore little resemblance to the country he had so gladly left in 1792. Then, he had wanted nothing more than to become an American and a republican. Now, when he sailed from New York on 2 June 1800, he confessed he found himself thoroughly confused.

Over the years, he had been offered money on several occasions by Robert Liston, the British Minister in Philadelphia. But he had always refused. What if he had been wrong, not merely about the strength of Jeffersonian democracy but about England and its present Tory administration? What if England was not the best of all possible worlds, being full of ancient corruption and 'The Thing', as well as French Jacobins and American Democrats? 'Very soon after my arrival in London,' Cobbett tells us, he was made aware of how important it was in various political and literary circles that he had been Peter Porcupine.

> I was invited to dine at MR. WINDHAM's, who was then Secretary of War, and did dine in the company of Mr. Pitt, who was very polite to me... I was well aware that Mr. Pitt never admitted newspaper writers to such an honour.

As A. J. P. Taylor says, in his fine essay on Cobbett: 'There is nothing more agreeable in life than to make peace with The Establishment – and nothing more corrupting.'[9]

Cobbett was told, in no uncertain terms, that his desire to be free and independent was highly eccentric and that the Administration (or 'The Thing', as he called it) expected him to build a Fleet Street newspaper career on their patronage alone. 'I tell you what, Cobbett,' journalist John Reeves told him, 'we have only two ways here; we must either *kiss* their arses or *kick* them; and you must make your choice at once.'[10] Thirty years later, Cobbett recalled: 'I resolved to kick.'

But that was not his immediate reaction. He continued for a long time to think like an American. 'I believed that independence was everything.' It was some years before the government saw Cobbett as anything more dangerous than too high a Tory or too zealous a supporter of the war against the French.

He began by selling and exporting other men's books and newspapers to America from an expensive address in Southampton Street, Strand. He was not successful. He had refused point blank to pay the Secretary of the Post Office, Francis Freeling, his customary rake-off for an export licence and, in consequence, ran quickly into debt. 'The business demanded thousands in place of my few hundred,' he says. He sold up at a considerable loss and moved to much cheaper premises at 183 Fleet Street, determined to beat 'The Thing'.

William Cobbett (1763–1835) published his *Political Register* mostly from 183 Fleet Street and later Bolt Court, but it was born at 15 Duke Street (Westminster) in 1802. Its circulation was 4,000 a week in 1805 and, according to Jeremy Bentham, rose to 'well above 60,000' in 1816.

By the start of 1802, he had managed to bring out the first number of his *Political Register*, that most famous of all political weeklies. It was an entirely new type of serious popular journalism and an immediate success, even at 1*s.* ½*d.* for each copy. Printed by T. C. Hansard of Peterborough Court, 'the very best printer in London' according to Cobbett, it aroused interest everywhere, as nothing had done since the days of Tom Paine ('Where is MY FRIEND Cobbett's paper?' asked the old King when he visited Cufnell's in 1804). It was heavily dependent on 'Letters to the Editor', most of which were either solicited or commissioned by Cobbett himself. It was remarkably well informed about what was really going on in government and about how much it would cost the taxpayer. It carried important State Papers in full, both foreign and domestic, most of which would have been denied to Fleet Street without the help of his highly-placed friend and fellow director, Mr William Windham. But, most innovative of all, the *Register* was written speakably, in what was rapidly becoming an American tradition.

As Henry Weisser has said: 'Quality was much less important to Cobbett than rapport with his readers.' Roughly, raucously, often raunchily, like the know-all in a tavern, Cobbett set up a button-holing dialogue with his readers. The Dutiful Town Crier, with all the official news and little else, had become the Tall Talesman with something under the counter for all the family. Deference was conspicuous by its absence: 'even a cat can look at a king where I come from', Cobbett seems to be saying. Democracy, like they are enjoying in America, will soon be available here – if we push hard enough. And, as for politics, that's generally a 'Knife and Fork' question, isn't it? Cobbett had no sympathy with the Whig Opposition in this area: 'It is the country that is now stirring. But does it stir for the OUTS? No, Sir: nor would it have stirred an inch for them if they had bawled "till Midsummer"' (2 March 1816). His ideas on reform were far more radical.

> 'What GOOD would a reform of Parliament do now? It would do away with the profligacy, bribery and perjury of elections, and do more for the morals of the people than has been done by all the Bible societies and all the schools that have ever been set on foot, and all the sermons that have ever been preached. [12 October 1816]

It would put an end to 'that accursed thing called Parliamentary interest. Promotions and honours in the army, the navy, the Church, the law, and in all other departments, would follow MERIT' (19 October 1816). And:

> A Reformed Parliament would not forget to enquire *why* Mr. Ponsonby and Lord Erskine receive four thousand a year each, and are to receive it for life; *why* Mr. Huskisson is always to receive twelve hundred pounds a year when he is not in an office which brings in more than that sum; *why* Mrs. Mallet du Pan and William Gifford are kept by the public; *why* the Seymours receive such immense sums, and the Somersets; *why* Lady Luisa Paget and numerous other dames of quality receive incomes out of the public taxes. [12 October 1816]

It was lively stuff, if somewhat ahead of its time. It was also dangerously misleading in its American assumptions. But it sold 'like pancakes, hot and hot', according to William Hazlitt,[12] who added, somewhat jealously; 'Fresh theories give Cobbett fresh courage. He is like a young and lusty bridegroom that divorces a favourite speculation every morning and marries a new one every night.' In other words, Cobbett was 'up to no good but the beat of his blood', and would not be able to stay the course. Hazlitt was eventually proved right. By November 1816, the *Register* was selling 40,000 copies a week (far more than *The Times* even on its best day) and, when a cheap edition was started at 2*d.*, this figure rose to 'well above 60,000', according to Jeremy Bentham.

In its new format the *Register* appeared as one large sheet of first quality paper with four wide columns. It left out the general news, which necessitated paying the large Stamp Tax, contained in the expensive edition (which continued), carrying only his gossipy, weekly letter and 'Letters to the Editor', to a completely new public. As Cobbett put it, on 16 November 1816:

> Two or three journeymen or labourers cannot spare a shilling and a halfpenny a week; but they can spare a halfpenny or three farthings each, which is not much more than the tax which they have to pay on a quid of tobacco. And besides the expense of the thing itself thus becomes less than the expense of going to a public house to hear it read. – Then there is the time for reflection, and the opportunity of reading over again, and of referring to interesting facts. The *children* will also have an opportunity of reading it... The *wife* can sometimes read, if her husband cannot. The women will understand the causes of their starvation and raggedness as well as the men and will lend their aid in endeavouring to effect the proper remedy. Many a father will, thus, I hope, be induced to spend his evenings at home, in instructing his children in the history of their misery, and in warning them into acts of patriotism.

This cosy fireside picture, drawn by Cobbett at the height of his considerable powers, was a prospect too awful for the government to contemplate. Early radicals, Anglo-French *philosophes* in particular, had talked over people's heads when holding forth about 'natural rights'. But Anglo-American Cobbett was something else. He really got through to them. The fellah has got to go! He comes here from America, unleashes the wildest kind of democratic tendencies, and is now directing them not merely against the government, but Parliament itself! 'Government by Journalism', his Jacobin friends called it! Whatever it was, it was quite intolerable and could only lead to anarchy. Fleet Street had spawned a terrible monster and must be punished. Habeas corpus was suspended and Cobbett, together with many others, threatened with arrest.

To everyone's surprise, Cobbett chose to flee to America. For him, there was to be no martyrdom. He had already tasted the the misery of Newgate Prison, back in 1810. Now, he was being threatened with transportation to Australia. He decided he preferred self-exile in comfort, with time off for good behaviour. Better the devil you know than seven years' hard labour in the Antipodes. Better to leave a legend than a dead end. He had established the divine right of media demagogues to speak for the people, with the arrogance of the rich, in the language of the poor. That was quite an achievement for a lad born to the Surrey plough. Imitating the loud, brash Cobbett manner, would become a full-time occupation for many in Fleet Street. Tom Paine may have provided the slogans, but William Cobbett had supplied the style and the tone for demotic newspaper writing.

Why Cobbett returned to England for the second time, in November 1819, we shall never know. It was probably a combination of boredom with farming on his Hyde Park Farm (later the birthplace of Franklin Delano Roosevelt) and curiosity about the political repercussions of the 'Peterloo Massacre', which occurred in Manchester in August of that year. He says he was also toying with the idea of launching a mass-produced daily, using *The Times*'s new steam press (if he could afford it) and turning the old *Register* into an evening paper. Nationwide publicity for this 'tentative' idea, he calculated, would be 'absolutely guaranteed' if he were to erect a large statue in Fleet Street to the late Mr Tom Paine and then exhibit his 'canonized bones' (dug up at dead of night from Paine's pauper grave in Brooklyn) to pay for it. 'It was a romantic idea,' says Hazlitt, generously,

> but doomed from the start. The fact is he *ratted* from his own project [the moment he arrived in Liverpool]. He found the thing not so ripe as he had expected. His heart failed him; his enthusiasm fled; and he made his retraction. No sooner did he reach London, than he made a speech to disclaim all participation in the political and theological sentiments of his late idol, [whose bones he left in some Liverpool boarding-house to shift for themselves!] and to place the whole stock of his admiration and enthusiasm towards him... to his having predicted the fate of paper money!

Meanwhile, in a Fleet Street physically unchanged since the Great Fire, and still without a purpose-built printing works in the immediate area (the first being James Moyes's Temple Printing Office in 1826), other personal forces were fighting for their professional lives. Richard Carlile, one of the most foolhardy of the Fleet Street Radicals, was now languishing in Dorchester Gaol. His eye-witness report of Peterloo, published in *Sherwin's Weekly Political Register* with great effect, had ensured his instant arrest.

Another eye-witness and his editor, John Tyas and Thomas Barnes of *The Times*, were also in deep trouble. Tyas was now barred from the House of Commons for his 'partisan' reporting of Peterloo. He had been the leading parliamentary reporter there since he came down from Cambridge in 1812. Barnes, his commissioning editor, was summoned to the Home Office, where, before a very full Cabinet Council, 'consisting, as well as I could distinguish with my nearsightedness, of Lord Liverpool, Lord Sidmouth, Lord Castlereagh, the Duke of Wellington, Lord Harrowby, the Chancellor of the Exchequer, Lord Bathurst, and another, I believe, Mr. Robinson', he was told 'sternly' to watch his step – 'an object in which it utterly failed'. He was now wholeheartedly in favour of reform and 'agin the Government'. Defiantly, he travelled to Oldham, together with his 'favourite' reporter, to insist on his paper's right to report the inquest on the Peterloo Massacre being held there. Lord Brougham journeyed over from York to advise him, bringing along a dossier on the 'knavish' Deputy Constable of Manchester, Joseph Nadin, which completely vindicated the reformers and 'damned the Government as despots'.

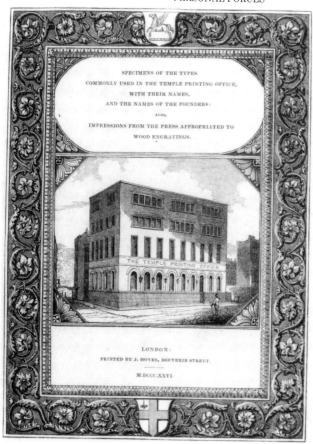

be attempted on grounds of good feeling or humanity.

A word on this part of the question, which concerns the capture of HUNT and those about him. Our readers will find amongst the names of the prisoners, that of a gentleman of the name of TYAS. Mr. TYAS went down from London to take notes of whatever he should see and hear, and report it for *The Times*. He is a gentleman of talent and education; nephew to an individual of great respectability in the town of Manchester, and, so far as we can judge from his preceding conduct towards this journal, about as much a Jacobin, or friend of Jacobins, as is Lord LIVERPOOL himself. Mr. TYAS had been very seriously indisposed from the day of his arrival at Manchester. Anxious, however, to discharge, in the most satisfactory manner, his duty to us and to the public, he determined to procure, if possible, a place near HUNT on the day of the meeting, for the sake of sparing his own infirm health, and for the greater facility of sending us a complete report. By what means he so unluckily succeeded in this purpose, as to be considered one of HUNT's party, we have yet no materials for conjecturing: but, greatly as we have been grieved for his sake by this accident, and severely as it has disappointed our hopes of affording more ample and perfect information to our readers, we mention the circumstance less as a subject of complaint with regard to our personal feelings, than as a mode of illustrating the manner in which those who acted for the magistrates thought fit to exercise the power, and to discharge the functions, assigned to them. Mr. TYAS, we have reason to know, was absolutely unacquainted with HUNT, at the moment of his entering Manchester: of what has since happened, we are as ignorant as the public at large.

But we revert to the more solemn question, of the legal

Two events now occurred which pushed Fleet Street closer to rebellion even more than the French Revolution. Together, they determined its public attitude towards government for the next century and a half. (Writing in 1976, Louis Heren, Deputy Editor and Foreign Editor of *The Times* in those days, summed up this 'traditional' attitude as follows: 'A good journalist should always be an adversary, eyeing those in positions of authority with the deepest scepticism if not suspicion.'[13]) The first was the 'infamous' Six Acts of 1819, which were aimed directly at Fleet Street's 'impertinence'. They constitute 'the historic high-water mark in repressive legislation' according to Lord Briggs, and united the press in opposition to ministerial government. The second was the 'Queen's Affair' of 1820, which nullified the deterrent effect of the Six Acts and unleashed violent political demonstrations in London, demanding to know 'Where's the injured Queen?' 'There was never an episode in British history more damaging to Royalty and its claims than the Queen Caroline Affair,' according to G. D. H. Cole, and the government's frenzied attempts to smother the popular interest aroused by it played straight into the hands of the new commercial press sensationalists. Not only did they greatly enlarge the huge discredit of the corrupt 'boroughmongering' system and spread anti-government feeling throughout the country. The bla-

Above Left James Moyes's prospectus for his Temple Printing Office (at the junction of Bouverie Street and Tudor Street) – probably the first to be designed as such.

Above Right When, in August 1819, *The Times* sent their best reporter, John Tyas, to cover a political meeting in St Peter's Fields, Manchester, it upset the authorities. It suggested not merely that *The Times* expected trouble (see above) but also that it was in league with the promoters of the meeting (untrue). Tyas was forced to complete his report in a prison cell and Thomas Barnes, his editor, was brought before a full Cabinet Council.

tant hypocrisy provoked hitherto servile London workers into pitched battles against the Life Guards sent to disperse them. Not surprisingly, the popular upsurge was never wholly under the control of the parliamentary reformers (except at the beginning), being led in the streets by labour leader, John Gast, the secretary of the shipwright's union, and in the radical press by William Cobbett, self-appointed speech-writer and press adviser to the Queen. 'They worked well together,' says labour historian, Iowerth Prothero, and almost produced a new political party, the Carolingians.

For the first time since Henry VIII, a profligate English king was forcing his ministers to do their utmost to get him a divorce regardless of public opinion. But they first had to deprive his Queen Caroline of her royal title! No newspaper could have resisted such a topic, particularly when it revolved around sex (and illicit sex at that). Indeed, only the *Morning Post* tried: 'Turn a deaf ear to your news-

Thomas Barnes, editor of *The Times* from 1817 to 1841, was a schoolfellow of Leigh Hunt at Christ's Hospital, a poet and drama critic, and an early contributor to the Hunts' *Examiner*.

paper *advocates*', the Queen was told. 'Their object is short and simple – the sale of *Seven Penn'orth*.' Most other newspapers came out lustily 'for the People and agin the Government', and stayed that way for years. It was the old royal road to popular success – an unfailing Fleet Street formula. This time it brought modernity to Fleet Street, or, as the critics would say, 'power without responsibility'. Peterloo was already history, even in that self-regarding paper of record, *The Times*. But Queen Caroline was news – hot news – from the second most important news source in the land, Windsor Castle. The *Morning Chronicle* reported that *everyone* pitied the ill-treated wife of the King: the *True Briton* dismissed him as 'incorrigible', and Cobbett as 'a wastrel with a *total disregard* to the opinions of the world'. Only a religious revival would be able to put any kind of brake on its full exploitation in the press.

A less deserving popular idol than Queen Caroline can hardly be imagined. But a large section of the public (encouraged by Methodists and Unitarians) was prepared to recognize her as a deeply wronged woman. Thomas Barnes, the first professional editor of *The Times*, was in no doubt (or moral concern) about her illicit love affair in Italy. He had been given all the gory details by his chief foreign correspondent, Henry Crabb Robinson, who moved in the most exalted circles.

The Times achieved yet another 'first' in journalism with the gentlemanly Henry Crabb Robinson (1775–1867), pioneer foreign correspondent (Germany, 1807) and 'special' (Peninsular War, 1808–9), who later served as foreign editor in Printing House Square.

75

Barnes's attitude towards both the story and the public was strictly business: 'When the legend becomes news, we print the legend.' He was quite prepared to mislead the general public in the interests of reform. He was further gratified to find that his daily circulation figures improved immediately – from 10,000 to 15,000.

Crabb Robinson was furious, accusing Barnes of shameful opportunism. Barnes's replies to his letters have not been preserved. But, we are safe in assuming they conveyed 'the essential Fleet Street' message most succinctly. Barnes was a realist. He was also 'devilish clever', according to that man-about-town and fashionable poet, Tom Moore:

> No, editors don't care a button,
> What false and faithless things they do,
> They'll let you come and cut their mutton,
> And then they'll have a cut at you.

Crabb Robinson, who had been in Paris during The Terror, was terrified of mob violence. Barnes, however, was eager to open up this Pandora's Box. (He later regretted it and reverted to his earlier Toryism, after the 'excesses'of the 1832 Reform Act.) Queen Caroline may be no better than she ought to be – but at least she was quiet about it! The King's sexual behaviour, on the other hand, was too well-known to be glossed over. It was bringing the whole institution of monarchy into disrepute.

With the start of the so-called 'Trial of the Queen' (the introduction in the House of Lords of a retrospective Bill of Pains and Penalties, to dissolve the marriage and deprive her of her royal title), 'the London newspapers [says G. A. Cranfield] ceased to be newspapers at all. They became scandal sheets, devoting page after page, and often the entire issue, to the trial, so that readers could wallow at length in hitherto unplumbed depths of obscenity and scurrility'.[14] (Which is not strictly true, but close enough. Some of the Restoration *Mercuries* had plumbed greater depths, and *The Times* at least continued to provide an unrivalled general news service.)

Cobbett's speech-writing for the Queen, and his powerful editorials in several newspapers as well as his own, 'turned her views into news and her pleas into commands', according to Thomas Creevey. Officially, she was advised what to say by Lord Brougham. But it was largely through Cobbett's 'handling' that she became 'the Queen of the Radicals' and 'leader of the Seditious Rabble'.[15] John Gast collected 29,786 signatures to a demand for the Bill's withdrawal, and organized a procession of artisans 'which made one continuous link' from Hyde Park to Brandenburgh House at Hammersmith (which was the Queen's residence at this time). Not surprisingly, the Bill was withdrawn before it could get to the House of Commons. People power had triumphed.

The climax came on 23 January 1821, just before Parliament met, when 63 addresses were presented to the government and many trades marched. There were public appearances by the Queen, which drew large crowds. There were also lost motions in the House to include a reference to the Queen in the Litany. But nothing happened quite the way it was supposed to happen: the authorities made certain of that. And climax turned to anti-climax when the Queen decided to accept an annuity of £50,000 from the government.

Interest in the Queen's cause revived in the spring, when the Coronation was announced. Radicals hoped she would go to Westminster Abbey, determined to enforce her claim to be crowned, and receive active support from the crowd. This the Queen proceeded to do, threading her way through great crowds gathered outside her lodgings and the Abbey on Coronation Day, 19 July 1821. People were noisily sympathetic but no move was made to help her when she was refused entry at each door of the Abbey because she had no ticket. No row ensued, no untoward 'happening' occurred: the Queen fainted prettily on the pavement and was persuaded to go home. Radical plans for a separate coronation of the Queen, revealed in *The Statesman* by Sir Francis Burdett, were abandoned when the Queen suddenly died on 7 August, 'to the joy of the King and the relief of the Government', as Burdett put it.

The whole business seemed to be over – and probably would have been, except for intervention by the London press. Caroline's wish was to be buried quietly in her native Brunswick. Fleet Street, almost in unison, demanded a public funeral. Nobody wholly accepted, or approved of, the official announcement regarding her death. It left 'foul play' rumours unscotched and totally disregarded public concern. Everybody (meaning Fleet Street) needed time to think about 'their loss', and when Cobbett suggested that 'the people's beloved body' should lie in state 'for several days' at the Guildhall, *en route* to Harwich, he was loudly and widely supported.

The government, however, was determined to prevent any such exhibition. They planned to rush the body, as near to a gallop as possible, northwards over the roof of London to the City Road and from there to the Harwich Road and the sea. It did not happen quite that way on the day. Londoners were up early and seemed to be very well informed about the intended route. The biggest crowd was at Marble Arch, where the journey northwards was supposed to begin, and there was a bloody clash at Cumberland Gate when the Life Guards arrived to clear the way. Shots were fired, two men were killed, sabres were used freely and many were wounded trying to stop the cortège reaching the Edgware Road. They failed to do this. But, after travelling barely a quarter of a mile northwards through milling crowds, the funeral procession was forced towards the City. Slowly, it moved eastwards, eventually passing down a closely-packed Fleet Street, through St Paul's Churchyard and Cheapside to Leadenhall Street, where it broke up in disorder.

The coffin went separately to Harwich by water transport provided by the City. The cortège proceeded by land on the following day. Sir Richard Baker, chief magistrate at Bow Street, had to resign in disgrace; Sir Robert Wilson, Command-

In 1808, aged 24, Leigh Hunt founded (with his brother John) the 'magnificently rebellious' *Examiner*. (Portrait by Samuel Laurence)

ing Officer of the Life Guards, was dismissed from the Army: and the press roundly condemned the government for its 'gross mishandling of the funeral'. Angrily, Joseph Nightingale, writing in *The Observer* Sunday newspaper, ended his eye-witness report: 'Such was the beggarly manner in which those who wielded the power of Great Britain, thought fit to dismiss from its shore the body of their late queen.' (His report was later included in his best-selling popular book, *The Public and Private Life of Queen Caroline*.)[16] It is a remarkable piece of observational reporting and well worth reading in its entirety, since it captures the 'Spirit of the Age' better than most and includes the names and ages of the two men shot at Cumberland Gate.

'From then on,' Cobbett generalized wildly, 'there were no longer any Tories!' What he meant was, there were only apprehensive politicians attempting to discover the minimal amount of reform they would have to concede to avoid a revolution. For reformers, their cause was 'like a snowball' gathering size and weight all the way down to the 1832 Reform Act. England for a time had been seriously threatened by what Lord Grey feared might easily become 'a Jacobin Revolution more bloody than that of France'. Lady Jerningham expressed a common fear when she said that the country was nearer to disaster than it had ever been since the time of Charles I. 'There is a new confidence about the future,' noted Leigh Hunt in *The Examiner* on 19 August 1821, 'especially in Fleet Street, which is defiantly in mourning. We must not fail her [i.e., the Queen] or the people.' Popular cries of a sell-out were already being anticipated and one can detect a rising note of fear among those journalists who might be held responsible.

Georgian London was a lawless place, especially in the overcrowded centre. There was violence to persons as well as property each time the military appeared on the streets. Between 1801 and 1831, Greater London had increased its population from 800,000 to 1,500,000. The increase was mainly to the boroughs of Southwark and Lambeth, where most of the clerical and artisan class lived. (There was also an increase of 115 per cent in St Pancras, Camden Town, Paddington, Kensington and Chelsea.) More and more people had to walk considerable distances to get to their work: an 8-mile tramp to Hampstead and back after work was nothing. There was no public transport (except for the very rich); there was hardly any local government, not even public facilities, and the streets stank. But there was invariably some kind of free entertainment in the West End.

Central London was gaslit very early in the century. It was also patrolled by the military, day and night. There were expensive shops to be gazed at in the newly-built Regent Street and 'funnymen' on every street corner. There were hundreds of stand-up drinking bars – and just as many armed private guards to keep the crowds moving, assisted by 'runners' and informers. Reform meetings, which began in the Charing Cross area around 6pm, would become rowdy and troublesome long before they emerged to march in the streets. They were entirely preoccupied with repressive measures and would react 'agin the Government' at the merest sight of a uniform, even one of Peel's uniformed police, instituted in 1829. Gendarmerie of any kind was bitterly resented. In 1833 a London jury, sitting on the death of three peelers killed in a reform riot, found it was justifiable homicide. The fact that they had been unarmed was dismissed as foolishness on their part.

Excited crowds, according to R. H. Mottram,[17] would often retreat to 'the sanctuary of Fleet Street' where, in that persistently notorious district of Whitefriars (roughly bounded by the Temple, Fleet Street, Bridge Street and the river), 'they would re-group, make new banners and re-emerge to do battle for Reform'. Temple Bar would be 'temporarily' closed to the pursuing military, and thus the 'ancient right of sanctuary' (going back to the time when there were protected monasteries in Fleet Street) became an additional factor in 'the hornpipe for Reform orchestrated by the London press' (Creevey). Many unemployed people came to believe, writes E. E. Kellett,[18] that:

Compositors' room in the Temple Printing Office, showing the extra-large windows at odds with the rest of the gloomy architecture.

the dark places of the earth might be full of cruelty but Fleet Street would let in the light, and the pen, more potent than the tree of Moses, would cleanse the waters of corruption. The demagogue and the oppressor would stand revealed together, and the Millennium would be at hand.

This was not simply popular superstition: it was almost 'government by Fleet Street', forcing the official government to consider most carefully all direct, anti-press action. Doubtless, you could still 'bribe or twist' the individual journalist. But, *pace* Humbert Wolfe, seeing what The Street could do unbribed, there was no occasion to. From now on, even flagrant sedition would be dependent for its identification on the co-operation of the jury. The government insisted, however, on the widening of Fleet Street. The City Fathers responded with alacrity, being equally fond of pageantry, widening it to 45 feet (14 metres) from 30 feet (9 metres) between Fleet Bridge and St Bride's, and removing the ornate conduit from the middle of the road to permit easier passage for the military. But nothing was done to restrain the Temple Bar gatekeepers from closing the main gate at night to all except 'bona fide visitors and residents'. Temple Bar, after all, was the traditional 'bawwier' between the City and the rest of the world.

The amazing success of Cobbett, with his vigorous and pellucid style of writing, and the earlier lesson taught by 'Junius', that anonymity can add force to invective, had not been lost on their successors. 'There is,' wrote Junius to his brother-journalist John Wilkes, 'something oracular in the delivery of my opinions. I speak from a recess which no human curiosity can penetrate. The mystery of Junius increases his importance.' The great Unknown[19] might have added that his importance was further increased by his habit (copied by Fleet Streeters generally) of always talking as if he knew everything.

Georgian editors may therefore be pardoned for believing that, by adding the anonymity of Junius to the popular appeal of Cobbett and by maintaining a pontifical attitude of infallibility, they might exert an almost unlimited power. It was an awesome discovery, made clear probably for the first time during the Caroline Affair, when 'audacity of censure' and 'exaggeration of flattery' by newspapers, especially *The Times*, contributed considerably to the weakness of government. But it was not an entirely happy discovery. *The Times* had been uniquely successful in its stand: it was determined not merely to report public opinion but to lead it. In one of his many impassioned and eloquent columns, Thomas Barnes, the first *Times* man who could properly be called 'editor' in the present-day sense, called upon 'the people' to 'petition, ay, thunder for reform', and unwittingly coined in the process a sobriquet for his paper which long outlived him: 'The Thunderer'. But Barnes was no populist; nor did he wish to be associated with so-called 'Rebel journalism'. He could not abide Cobbett. The *Political Register* seemed to him to have profited by French information, perhaps even by French gold. (It was not true, though Cobbett did later write for a French newspaper, recommended by Chateaubriand.) Barnes agreed with James Mill, the stern father of John Stuart Mill, that it was not 'good policy' to give the power of teaching the people to persons violating the law. Cobbett was a dangerous demagogue, and the only belief they had in common was that English dishonour abroad and distress at home were two aspects of the same problem – the corruption of the boroughmongers.

The cat of public opinion was now well and truly out of the bag, exciting everybody at all levels of society and running wild. Unrest was general and even insurrection seemed likely. What was needed more than anything else, in Barnes's view, was a period of stability and calm, so that the political education of the masses could proceed in an orderly manner. Like John Reith, chief architect of the BBC in the twentieth century, Barnes was a rigid (if not a frigid) paternalist who insisted on ruling alone. He knew what his people wanted and it was not demagoguery or even readable politics. It was functional information to protect themselves from the abuse of power by the legislators. It may involve liberty, in a limited sense, but not fraternity and certainly not equality.

Barnes's idea of public information was public instruction. It had nothing to do with democratization, which could only have a destabilizing effect on the country. Like most of the professional middle class, of which he was a part, Barnes dreaded mob violence more than anything. He was confirmed in this view, first by the aftermath of the Caroline Affair, and then by the Chartist movement, which began in 1833 led by wild men like Bronterre O'Brien crying 'sell-out'. By the time of his death in 1841 (having written most of Peel's famous Tamworth Manifesto without acknowledgement, and made deals with most members of the new Reform Parliament) Barnes had become, according to the Lord Chancellor, the most powerful man in the country. He had also turned *The Times* completely away from Cobbett's New Journalism, with all that it implied, and the Walter family would

John Thadeus Delane, editor of *The Times*, 1841–77. A social eminence as well as consummate journalist, Delane formed a formidable alliance with his proprietors (John Walter II and III) in spearheading the newspaper industry as 'the Fourth Estate'.

make sure it stayed that way as long as they remained in ownership. 'Mr Barnes sought certain changes in the law and constitution of this country and succeeded. Content with that success, he paused, without seeking further change... This is the only conduct deserving the praise of firmness and consistency' (Barnes's obituary in *The Standard*, 10 May 1841).

'Cheap news' in a cheap, typographical setting may suit the French (Serrière's *Le Petit Journal* was all the rage in Paris) and the Americans (Moses Beach was making the first newspaper fortune with his penny *New York Sun*), but it must be resisted by all 'serious' newsmen. It was the role of the press as a critic rather than as a potential manipulator of mass circulations which was to be emphasized here in the 1850s and 1860s. And when Dasent, the manager of *The Times* (together with Barnes's successor, John Thadeus Delane), claimed it was 'an advantage to con-fine the newspaper press as much as possible in the hands of a few persons with

large capitals', hinting at the 'gentlemanly' status of most 'responsible' newspaper proprietors and the irresponsibility of everyone else, he was not merely seeking special trading protection for *The Times*. He was proposing the abandonment of united action 'agin the government', and the resumption of the old class divisions.

There should be no 'poor man's history of laws, customs, institutions and opinions', as suggested by Albany Fonblanque in *The Examiner* (10 February 1833). The newspaper should remain limited in its appeal; its price prohibitive and its range of information restricted to middle class concerns. Cheap 'trash' on a Sunday was one thing: deplorable but presumably necessary to placate tired workers. But giving them functional news would be like giving away the vote. As for independence, the only independence that mattered was that from advertisers: any other kind would only make enemies. According to *The Spectator* (founded in

William Howard Russell (knighted in 1895) was the standard-bearer of *Times* special correspondents, against whose achievements all successors have been measured. Here is the famous photo taken in the Crimea by Roger Fenton, a pioneer in the parallel field of press photography.

1828), independence was: 'An Ishmael, with its hand against every man, it finds every man against it.' Delane agreed. Henceforward, *The Times* would be 'a Tory island in a sea of Liberalism', wielding power primarily from within the Cabinet itself, but also through its well-connected, 'ambassadorial' foreign correspondents.

William Howard Russell (1820–1907), for example, was able to perform journalistic miracles in the Crimea, 'with little more than a soft Irish brogue, a skilful pen, and a gambling connection with the young Prince of Wales.'[20] When Russell fell ill with trench fever, Thomas Chenery, *The Times*'s Constantinople correspondent, took over, exposing the horrors of the British hospital at Scutari and making Florence Nightingale immortal. Chenery (who succeeded Delane) was also a Professor of Arabic at Oxford and travelled everywhere 'like an Ambassador-without-Portfolio'. He, 'more than anyone', set the roving style for *Times* men, and was remembered with awe by Henri de Blowitz, the 'Prince of Journalists' and Paris correspondent, whose most famous coup was the revelation of the whole of the Berlin Treaty of 1878, seized from beneath the noses of the signatories while the ink was barely dry.

But Russell's dispatches earned him no official thanks. The Queen raged against 'the infamous attacks against the army which have disgraced our newspapers'. The Prince Consort, deeply involved in the running of the army, declared that 'the pen and ink of one miserable scribbler is despoiling the country'. Government spokesmen continued to deny that anything had gone seriously wrong and the War Office began drafting orders for the expulsion of correspondents whose writings might help the enemy – until a *Times* leader of 23 December 1854, followed by similar attacking leaders at regular intervals into the New Year, provoked a motion in the House of Commons from radical MP J. A. Roebuck (on 23 January 1855) asking for an inquiry 'into the condition of our Army before Sebastopol'. This amounted to a vote of no confidence in the government. Three hundred and five members voted for the motion and only 148 against. The government resigned and Lord Palmerston, over 70 but still very vigorous, became Prime Minister.

More than any other single factor, it was Russell's dispatches (coupled with back-room dealing by Delane) that had brought this about. 'It was you who turned out the Government,' the Duke of Newcastle, Aberdeen's War Secretary, told Russell in the Crimea a few months later. Other triggers were involved, of course – the inherent weakness of the Aberdeen coalition and the prestige of *The Times* – but few journalists in history can claim to have exerted such a direct influence on great events. It was an important moment in the history of 'new' Fleet Street and a signal success for public service journalism. Incidentally, it took 19 days (on average) for Russell's uncensored dispatches to reach London from the Crimea – which is three days fewer than were needed for heavily censored newsfilm to reach UK television screens during the Falklands War of 1982.

To *The Times*, comments Lord Briggs, 'even the secrets of the Palace were open'

was a plain to charge over, before the enemy's guns were reached, of a mile and half in length. At 11.10 our Light Cavalry brigade rushed to the front. They numbered as follows, as well as I can ascertain :—

				Men.
4th Light Dragoons	...	...	...	118
8th Irish Hussars	...	...	...	104
11th Prince Albert's Hussars	...	...	130
13th Light Dragoons	...	...	...	110
17th Lancers	...	...	...	145
Total ...	...	...		607 sabres.

The whole brigade scarcely made one effective regiment, according to the numbers of continental armies; and yet it was all we could spare. As they passed towards the front, the Russians opened on them from the guns in the redoubts on the right, with vollies of musketry and rifles they swept proudly past glittering in the morning sun in all the pride and splendour of war. We could scarcely believe the evidence of our senses! Surely that handful of men are not going to charge an army in position? Alas! it was but too true— their desperate valour knew no bounds; and far, indeed, was it removed from its so-called better part—discretion. They advanced in two lines, quickening their pace as they closed towards the enemy—a more fearful spectacle was never witnessed than those who, without the power to aid, beheld, their heroic countrymen rushing to the arms of death. At the distance of 1,200 yards the whole line of the enemy belched forth, from 30 iron mouths, a flood of smoke and flame, through which hissed the deadly balls. The flight was marked by instant gaps in our ranks, by dead men and horses, by steeds flying wounded or riderless across the plain. The first line is broken, it is joined by the second, they never

The Charge of the Light Brigade: part of Russell's dispatch from the Crimea. (*The Times*, 13 November 1854)

The most honoured name in early American press photography was Mathew Brady, and this is his version of Russell when both were covering the American Civil War. Russell's strong support for the rebel South made his writings as unpopular with the British government as his dispatches from the Crimea had been.

and he tells the story of how Lord Granville, entrusted by the Queen to form a government instead of Palmerston in 1859, gave a detailed account of the interview to Delane. Printed the following day, it greatly annoyed the Queen who naturally explained: 'Who am I to trust?' Granville denied that he had communicated anything to Delane. He claimed that *The Times*'s report had been drawn up 'in the usual vulgar, inflated manner' based on information received from leaky Cabinet friends. In fact, he had written to Delane immediately after seeing the Queen and the leakage was his own. Delane did not reveal this, and the truth only came out 30 years after Delane's death in 1879.[21]

But *The Times* was monopolizing too much of the newspaper scene and Fleet Street was beginning to resent it. 'What happens', W. R. Greg asked in 1855, 'when one single journal so monopolises the public ear and fills the public eye that other organs can scarcely be seen or heard?' Greg's uncompromisingly bold answer to his carefully aimed question was widely applauded:

> The republic of letters becomes a despotism, and menaces us with the evils attaching themselves to autocracy in all its forms … It is as if one senator held the proxies of 400 absentee members of the Lower House; and decided on his own responsibility the vote of an Assembly. *The Times*, it is notorious, has reached this extraordinary and dangerous eminence.[22]

Still on the attack, and introducing a new note about pluralism, Greg went on to speculate that 'the last alteration of the Stamp Duty [1855] would destroy most of Fleet Street,' let into London a whole host of cheap, provincial newspapers, and 'only turn to the profit of autocratic power' (i.e. *The Times*). Greg was, of course, completely wrong about Fleet Street. The credibility of the press did not lie in its apparent independence from the party political machine. It lay in its increasing ability to become the eyes and ears of the general public. The total abolition of the so-called 'Taxes on Knowledge' entirely altered the economics of newspaper distribution. It also brought 'papers for the million' into view for the very first time.

But Greg was right about *The Times*, at least in the immediate future. It continued to be necessary to look like *The Times*, if you wished to be taken seriously; and *The Times*'s circulation continued to rise, from 40,000 in 1851 (when it cost 5*d*.) to 70,000 in 1861 when it cost 3*d*. – the number of advertisements increasing proportionately. Matters only became difficult for *The Times* when its proud owners, the Walter family, lost heart. It was not the breaking of its monopoly, nor even the success of the despised penny newspaper, which caused this. It was simply the failure of George Buckle, a brilliant Oriel scholar who had succeeded to the editor's chair at the tender age of 29, to consult the family before involving them in a legal action which cost them £200,000. This was in 1889 when, for the first time that century, *The Times* recorded a deficit of £13,335. It never really recovered. In the next century it was to have five owners.

Ironically, while Greg was writing his famous critique of the 'monopolist' *Times* at its peak of perfection, its greatest competitor and monopoly breaker, *The Daily Telegraph*, was being born.[23] The first issue of *The Daily Telegraph and Courier* (as it was originally called) is dated Friday, 29 June 1855. It was founded by Lt.-Col. Arthur Sleigh 'to air some personal grievances' (according to Adrian Lighter) over his treatment by the Duke of Cumberland, who later became Commander-in-Chief of the Army. It was hardly more than a rich man's toy until it was taken over by its chief creditor, Joseph Moses Levy, printer-editor and proprietor of *The Sunday Times* in Shoe Lane. But it gave four six-column pages for 2*d*. 'The matter was good,' says Stanley Morison, 'the paper was good – and it looked anything but cheap.' With issue no. 45 (20 August 1855) the heading was simplified into one main line, *The Daily Telegraph*. With no. 57, the paper was transferred to Levy, and on 16 September 1855 (no. 69), London was given its first morning paper at the sensational price of 1*d*.

Setting the seal on his achievement in developing *The Daily Telegraph* from its shaky launch in 1855 to its undisputed 'largest circulation in the world', Edward Levy-Lawson became the 1st Baron Burnham in 1903. This is how Max Beerbohm saw him.

Henri Georges Stefan Adolphe Opper de Blowitz. When J. B. Guth pictured this larger-than-life *Times* man for *Vanity Fair* in 1889, Blowitz was at the height of his fame.

Twenty-five years earlier, in June 1832, Edward Bulwer had shocked the House by asking: 'Why is truth confined to the rich? Is it not time to consider whether the printer and his types may not provide better for the peace and honour of a free state, than the gaoler and the hangman?' Printer Levy was now in a position to reassure the House that his kind of cheapness was next to godliness; that there was no need to fear licentiousness from a 'free trade' daily paper 'conducted with a high tone'; and that 'Americanisms in lay-out' would not be permitted to lead to republicanism along American lines, not in *The Daily Telegraph*, anyway!

'The working man too will feel assured,' said Levy paternally in his first editorial, 'that we consider he is deserving of having laid before him a newspaper compiled with a care which places it in the Hamlet and secures its perusal in the Palace.' Such claims (as the 4th Lord Burnham, Levy's greatgrandson, pointed out much later) were 'somewhat' over-ambitious: the Palace had certainly not been won over, and most of the Hamlets were waiting for Harmsworth. But all that lay in between was available, particularly 'virtuous publicans and intelligent greengrocers' (Sala). 'Pre-eminently the "Cockney" newspaper,' H. W. Massingham called the *Telegraph* in 1892, meaning that lower middle-class London had taken it to its heart. Small advertisements were the life-blood of such a paper – even if the *Telegraph*'s box number invention managed to exclude all those unable to write!

There was also some truth in its announcement in October 1855 that: 'people will no longer have to buy the day before yesterday's *Times*... they can have a first-class newspaper upon their breakfast table as well as the rich. The price of *The Daily Telegraph* places it within the reach of every man.' Levy's son, Edward, who changed his name to Levy-Lawson and his religion to Christianity, was effectively editor and proprietor of the paper until 1903. (Then aged 70, he was raised to the peerage as Lord Burnham.) A quick, capable journalist of the campaigning variety, he confirmed the worst fears of the genteel by deliberately copying the sensational catch-penny techniques of the 'infamous' *New York Herald* (founded by Scots-born James Gordon Bennett in 1835). He 'proudly' went halves with Bennett in financing Stanley's search for Livingstone 'in darkest Africa', but deferentially 'Englished' his famous probing interviews so that he might visit 'titled celebrities' in the 'privacy of their homes'. Typical early headlines read: 'Extraordinary Discovery of a Man-Woman in Birmingham', 'Felonious Assault on Young Female', 'Shocking Occurrence: Five Men Smothered in a Gin Vat'.

Unfortunately, Levy-Lawson was hampered by lack of personal charisma and social confidence, to such an extent that subordinates sometimes dominated him and the paper. When Thornton Hunt (son of Leigh Hunt) was chief leader writer, for example, he overruled the policies of the proprietor. This was not, as the editor of *Truth*, Henry Labouchere, asserted, because Levy-Lawson possessed fewer pol-

To achieve a mass circulation *The Daily Telegraph* installed a ten-feed printer in 1860 in their new offices at 135 Fleet Street. (From *The Illustrated London News*.)

itical ideas than 'a vendor of fried fish in Petticoat Lane'. It was, at least in part, owing to racial prejudice. Labouchere attacked him regularly, in vicious anti-Semitic terms and called him Judas for betraying Gladstone and the Liberals in 1866 – a quarrel that culminated in a fist-fight outside the Beefsteak Club. And the *Telegraph*'s best writer, George Augustus Sala (1828–1895), would sometimes storm drunkenly into Levy-Lawson's office bawling: 'You bladdy Jew, give me some money.'[24]

Piers Brendon writes:

> It was actually Sala's personality more than Levy-Lawson's which pervaded *The Telegraph*. A colourful exhibitionist (second to none in Fleet Street, before or since), he possessed a massive nose which was said to be Fleet Street's most prominent landmark. It was inflamed by alcohol and had been split down the middle during a brawl in a brothel catering for his taste in flagellation.[25]

George Augustus Sala was first and foremost a *Daily Telegraph* man, but he also contributed 'Echoes of the Week' to *The Illustrated London News* for more than 25 years. He was the founder president of the Press Club. This 1875 drawing is by 'Ape' from *Vanity Fair*.

But Sala was also an extraordinarily accomplished journalist-of-all-work. His versatility can be gauged from this message which Levy-Lawson sent him in 1881: 'Please write a leader on Billingsgate and the price of fish, and start for St Petersburg this evening.' Long after Sala's death, according to John Merry Le Sage, his spirit seemed to haunt the new *Telegraph* building in Peterborough Court, 'a monstrous rookery with a stylish front for the advertisers,' opened in July 1882. (From 1857 to 1882, the *Telegraph* offices were in the 'tenement and shop known as No. 253 Strand in the Parish of St Clement Danes in the City and Liberty of Westminster', according to its 'birth certificate', a legal indenture beautifully hand-inscribed in Indian ink on two large sheets of vellum, dated 17 February 1857.)

Fleet Street itself was in an almost constant state of widening and realignment: 'a babel of competitive roarings'. Between 1880 and 1914, almost the whole[26] of its south side east of the Temple was set back. This prompted much rebuilding, with small offices for provincial papers strong among new tenants along the frontage, and larger offices for major London newspapers and printers in redeveloped Whitefriars. There was also the removal of Temple Bar, stone by stone, to an estate in Hertfordshire, and the introduction of horse-drawn omnibuses running on rails from Ludgate Hill to Charing Cross. There was rebuilding all round St Paul's; the long-drawn-out construction of Ludgate Circus, the widening of Farringdon Street following the 'burial' of the river Fleet; and the laying out of a grid of short commercial streets on the site of the City Corporation Gasworks and 'ricketty rookeries' south of Tudor Street.

By this time, the *Telegraph* had become, in Labouchere's graphic phrase, 'full of senile adulation for the powers that be'. Levy-Lawson was certainly not qualified to succeed Delane as doyen of Fleet Street. And neither, despite his superlative gifts as a popularizer, was W. T. Stead, editor of the *Pall Mall Gazette* from 1883 to 1889. He was considered by most of his Fleet Street contemporaries to be 'too much of a fanatic to be a good journalist – and too good a journalist to be a

good fanatic' (T. P. O'Connor). Stead was continually dreaming the impossible dream of a fiercely independent daily newspaper that would have clarity, judgement, patterned structure and beauty of appearance. It would read like a magazine, always be in the thick of the fight for democracy, and possess a staff 'prepared to live dangerously so that people could live more fully'.[27] It was a wonderfully far-sighted idea, but one which would be opposed at every level by the economic forces gathering strength and purpose in the City of London.

'The Guv'nor', as Levy-Lawson was called, did little to modernize his plant or his paper – apart from installing electric lighting in the early 1880s and a 'reserve printing works' at the corner of Tudor Street and Carmelite Street in 1886. It was, therefore, ill-equipped to resist the *Daily Mail*'s challenge at the end of the century, when the mass-production methods of the vigorous and 'completely unbuttoned' American newspaper industry were translated in earnest to the small family business concerns of Fleet Street. This, of course, was the start of a long process, still to run its course, and one that would, by a technical paradox, bring the newspaper much closer in the manner of its production to its twentieth-century rivals, radio and television. But it was seen by contemporaries as the beginning of the end of Fleet Street.

'The Philistines have captured the Ark of the Covenant (i.e., the printing press) and have learnt how to work their own miracles through its terrible power', declared that young Liberal historian, G. M. Trevelyan, writing in 1901.[28] It was all the fault of those 'unprincipled grocers', the new press lords, who were recklessly selling newspapers like soap! To exploit popular ignorance and weakness

All the principal participants in the Berlin Congress in 1878, headed by Bismarck, Disraeli and Count Karolyi of Italy, signed this fan for Blowitz.

91

was no more worth considering than living on the profits of disorderly houses! We should tell it like it is, not like it isn't!

Later, in 1921 (just before Captain John Reith of the brand-new British Broadcasting Company began to think along similar, paternalist, lines), H. W. Massingham looked back with longing to the Golden Age before Northcliffe, 'when papers were organs of opinion and Fleet Street was more or less a habitation of the mind'.[29] Like Jimmy Porter in *Look Back in Anger*, Massingham was 'crying for the Moon'. In 1928, John Francis Gore called Fleet Street 'a street of hasty judgement, of distorted truth, of elastic morality, of easy conviction'[30] – which is a far cry from 'to enlighten, to civilise, and to morally transform the world' (James Grant, editor of the *Morning Advertiser* from 1850 to 1871).

It was no accident, therefore, that the first newspaper revolution in modern times (the introduction of the linotype machine in 1886) did next to nothing for journalism. It was not intended to: the new production process was much more important commercially than the journalistic product. The same thing is true of the second revolution, computerization, which occurred in the USA in the mid-1960s and in the UK in the mid-1970s. But the introduction of mechanical typesetting into Fleet Street during the 1890s (a decade after it had become common usage in Chicago, as well as on the eastern seaboard) meant regress rather than progress as far as public service was concerned. It meant trivialization, fragmentation, and the worst kind of sensationalism, 'which you don't have to employ but which sells newspapers better if you do' (Stead).

The offices of the *Morning Advertiser* at 127 Fleet Street – the first daily published regularly in the street itself, from 1815 to 1929. The site was then sold to the *Daily Express*. The *Morning Advertiser* is still the daily for the licensed trade.

Instead of shaping and making public opinion in the Liberal image – which had been the purpose of most middle-class newspaper owners from Peterloo onwards – it suddenly became necessary to maximize profits and exploit the readership wherever possible. Why? Because the huge capital outlay needed to transform a largely 'class' press into a 'mass' press had turned Fleet Street into a 'hard sell' business community where only the most single-minded businessman could possibly hope to survive. Paternalism had become very expensive, uphill work, producing small thanks in the way of votes and circulation figures where the readership was unknown and unappreciated. But pandering to popular prejudice against 'rich toffs' (or even Jews) produced mass votes as well as mass circulations. It was also much easier to do than investigative journalism, especially if you hired some of the new, professionally-trained, 'formula news-writers' to do it, rather than 'inspired amateurs' from Oxbridge.

By the 1880s, according to Harold Spender, 'Fleet Street hated the Universities. They despised our degrees; scorned our knowledge and mocked at our modest river prides.'[31] Young Philip Gibbs merely added to this list when he remarked: 'It was de rigueur to be dressed for business in frock coats with full skirts, striped peg-top trousers (not baggy at the knees), a tie like a stock (still worn by Hannen Swaffer in the 1930s), and a high topper worn at a slight angle.'[32] Northcliffe would be rid of all this: he 'more naturally judged good journalism by reference to the circulation books'.[33] He looked round anxiously for a different kind of style,

one that would sell newspapers in large numbers to an audience deaf to these exhortations to become good Liberals. He found it in America, pioneered by Joseph Pulitzer and 'putrified to a fine ripeness'[34] by William Randolph Hearst.

The newly erected 'French classical' *Morning Post* building, No. 1 Aldwych/346 Strand, in 1908. The owner, Lord Glenesk, died the same year, and control of the paper passed to his daughter, Lady Bathurst.

5 'A Babel of Competitive Roarings'

(Frederick Greenwood, 1890)

Once the press had been deregulated in 1855, following the abolition of the newspaper stamp duty and government encouragment of free trade, a swarm of new publications emerged aggressively from 'holes' in Fleet Street producing a veritable babel of competitive roarings. Each one tried hard to 'scoop' the others with sensational revelations, 'which you don't have to use but which sell newspapers better if you do' (W. T. Stead) – and street sales suddenly became more important than subscription sales for proprietors tempted by the lucrative prospect of producing 'papers for the millions'.

Yours very sincerely
James Grant

James Grant edited the *Morning Advertiser* for the Society of Licensed Victuallers for 21 years. He widened its scope to include general news, and in 1858 was the first London editor to accept Reuter's agency service. Adopting an independent stance, and building on its popularity with publicans and coffee-house keepers, the *Morning Advertiser* was able to claim a circulation second only to that of *The Times*.

Opposite Top   In 1859 Sala published *Twice Round the Clock*, a reworking of an old journalistic idea suggested by Charles Dickens. This book illustration by William McConnell shows 'The Sub-Editors' Room'.

Opposite Bottom   '*The Times* Office, 1858', another McConnell drawing in *Twice Round the Clock*.

MIDNIGHT: THE SUB-EDITOR'S ROOM.

PUBLICATION OF THE "TIMES" NEWSPAPER: INSIDE THE OFFICE.

MR. J. A. MACGAHAN
Daily News (With the Russians)

MR. F. VILLIERS
Artist of *The Graphic* (With the Russians)

MR. ARCHIBALD FORBES
Daily News (With the Russians)

MR. MELTON PRIOR
Artist of the *Illustrated News* (With the Turks)

MR. CAMILLE BARRÈRE
Manchester Guardian and *Rep. Francaise* (With the Turks)

96

MR. HENRY DYMOND
Morning Advertiser (With the Turks)

LIEUT.-COL. BRACKENBURY
Times (With the Russians)

MR. W. KINGSTON
Daily Telegraph (With the Turks)

Above 'Burial of Mr Cameron, Special Correspondent of *The Standard*': artist's impression by Melton Prior, one of his pallbearers after the Battle of Abu Kru in the Sudan. As well as individual memorials to Russell, Forbes and Prior himself, there are collective memorials in the crypt of St Paul's Cathedral to the five 'specials' killed in the Sudan and the 13 lost in the South African War. (*The Illustrated London News*, 28 February 1885)

Individual portraits 'Newspaper correspondents' from *The Graphic*, 25 August 1877. The Balkan Wars of 1876 and 1877 and the Russo-Turkish War of 1877 captured popular imagination, and fuelled anti-Turkish feeling in the West. The Irish-American correspondent Januarias A. MacGahan, reporting for the *Daily News*, wrote: 'I fear I am no longer impartial, and I am certainly no longer cool.'

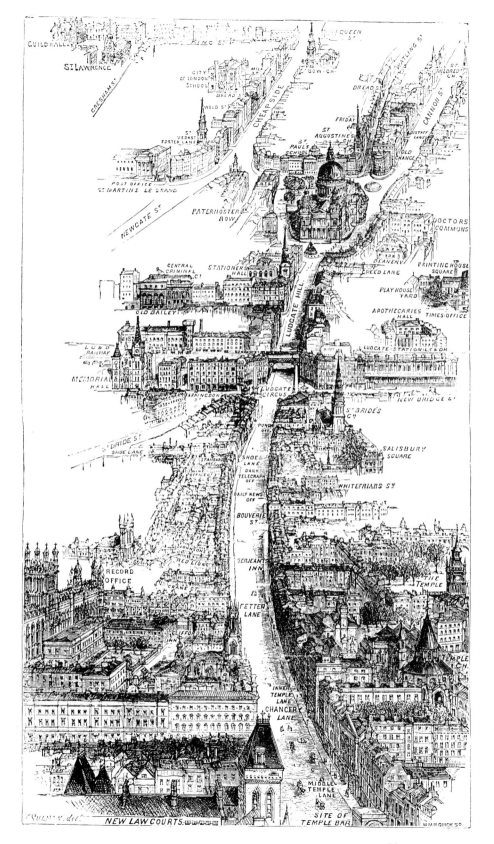

Opposite   Herbert Fry's classic work *London: Illustrated by 20 Bird's-Eye Views of its Principal Streets* features, in this edition, *The Daily Telegraph* in Fleet Street itself, the *Daily News* in Bouverie Street, *The Standard* in Shoe Lane, *The Times* in Printing House Square, and in the foreground 'the new Law Courts', opened in 1882. The obelisks in Ludgate Circus commemorated John Wilkes and Robert Waithman, a Fleet Street trader, as 'champions of freedom'.

Left   South side scene: from left, Falcon Court and 32–30 Fleet Street, 1883.

Below   'Fleet Street in election time: the rush for newspapers'. (*The Illustrated London News*, 1885)

99

Above Miss Harriet Martineau, political pundit of the *Daily News*, wrote some 1,600 leaders long before there were women's pages or even bylined women correspondents, such as Mrs Emily Crawford, Paris correspondent of the *Daily News* in the 1880s.

Opposite Some leading proprietors, editors and other newspaper personalities of the 1880s. Left to right (top): W. H. Mudford, *The Standard*; Edmund Yates, *The World*; 3rd Earl of Malmesbury, *Truth*; Frederick Greenwood, *The St James's Gazette*; G. A. Sala, *The Daily Telegraph*; (centre): John Walter III, *The Times*; (lower row): J. M. Robinson, the *Daily News*; John Lash Latey, *The Illustrated London News*; F. C. Burnand, *Punch*; W. L. Thomas, *The Graphic*; Edward Lloyd, *The Daily Chronicle*. (Origin unknown: reproduced from *Journalism Studies Review*, No. 2, 1977).

Left The *Daily News* first occupied this building in Bouverie Street in 1885. It was embellished by small busts of celebrities like Charles Dickens, the newspaper's first, short-stay, celebrity editor.

Above Francis Carruthers Gould, the first staff cartoonist on a daily newspaper (the *Pall Mall Gazette*, 1888). When George Newnes founded *The Westminster Gazette*, a Liberal evening paper, in 1893, F. C. G. became its political cartoonist, and three years later the assistant editor.

Left Carruthers Gould's bookplate. Gould rides past Westminster, with the heads of politicians of the day hung from his pen.

Opposite General view of Fleet Street looking east to Ludgate Hill, *c*.1880.

Above Ludgate Circus *en fête* for Queen Victoria's Golden (1887) or Diamond (1897) Jubilee. On
the corner of Fleet Street is Ludgate House, erected in 1873 as Thomas Cook & Son's head office,
hitherto in smaller premises across the street. The frontage as later extended was – and still is –
embellished with a profusion of statuary: heads representing the races of the world; cherubs,
globes, maps, ships and trains to symbolize how Cook's served that world. Many famous
correspondents started their adventures here.

Opposite The Street, again looking east. *c.*1900 (photo by F. J. Mortimer). In left foreground is
the entrance to Wine Office Court, the offices of the Press Association, and the Cheshire Cheese.

6   Pimps or Pimpernels?

T he New Journalism debate that raged for months in the heart of London's clubland a century ago was not really about journalism at all. It was about democracy and the disturbing political ideas of a messianic newspaper editor called William Thomas Stead. It may have started with Stead's 'Maiden Tribute of Modern Babylon', in July 1885, an exposé of juvenile prostitution proclaiming that 'the hour of Democracy has struck', which offended many clubmen.[35] But it only became a white-hot row after several other political writings had also fallen from the magisterial pen of Stead – whom God had called to 'the only true throne in England',[36] namely, the *Pall Mall Gazette* editor's chair.

In May 1886 Stead's bold article, 'Government by Journalism', appeared in the *Contemporary Review*. In November an even bolder sequel appeared, entitled 'The Future of Journalism'. Both articles made large claims regarding the public service duties of an editor, and a brisk national debate ensued over 'one of the most audacious assertions of press power ever made in Britain'.[37] Gentlemanly discussion turned into a slanging match, however, when that scholar-poet Matthew Arnold chose to attack Stead and his New Journalism in the *Nineteenth Century* magazine a year later in May 1887. Arnold declared himself 'deeply disturbed' by the verbal and visual crudities of the New Journalism. He argued that they were not merely culturally offensive to all right-thinking members of society; they were actually misleading the untutored minds of Britain's emerging democracy. Stead's newspaper, he insisted, 'throws out assertions at a venture, simply because it wishes them to be true'. It also, he said, gives them (i.e., the masses) 'a disposition to be featherbrained' – presumably about matters that did not properly concern them – 'just as the upper class is disposed to be selfish in its politics and the middle class narrow'.[38]

Arnold was right, of course. Stead's campaigns, or escapades, as he called them, were misleading. They were also disturbing the balance of Victorian society. It can be argued that he was 'up to no good but the beat of his inky blood'.[39] It can also be said that his rabble-rousing campaigns were giving simple folk the idea that more things could be achieved by 'a newspaper with a conscience'[40] than was constitutionally possible or even politically permissible. But if Arnold was partly

right, he was more generally wrong. He was completely wrong about Stead's motives, which were humanitarian rather than commercial. He was also wrong about his effect on ordinary working people, which was uplifting rather than injurious. Stead's highly readable journalism was popular not because it was sensationally vulgar and morally offensive, but because it was 'radiant, radical and rebellious'.[41] It was capable of ennobling as well as entertaining. It was also managing to talk about democracy democratically, like nobody since William Cobbett or Tom Paine, and it was this aspect of his writing that was having the unbalancing effect.

Stead was no mere 'sentimental radical' like the late Charles Dickens.[42] Stead was a campaigner to be feared. He didn't mind breaking the law if it was necessary, and he positively revelled in going to prison if only because it proved his point about there being a political cover-up.[43] He was not afraid of any bureaucrat who tried to block his inquiries. He had a powerful friend, Lord Esher, who had access to the primary sources and the secret Treasury accounts.[44] He was simply asking for some old-fashioned Christian justice and found talking about the equality of Christians in the eyes of God a most fearsome combination in a society that prided itself on its religiosity! He declared himself to be God's weapon on earth, a man with a mission. He had come down from the north of England to offer the world much more than 'a peep-show' and an opposition argument to Disraeli's 'progressive Toryism'.[45]

Stead had gone to London to expose corruption and criminal neglect or 'private

W. T. Stead: an early Downey photo (1893), taken just before he sailed to America for the first time.

107

THE PALL MALL GAZETTE

An Evening Newspaper and Review.

No. 6336.—VOL. XLII.   *MONDAY, JULY 6,* 1885.   *Price One Penny.*

"WE BID YOU BE OF HOPE."

THE Report of our Secret Commission will be read to-day with a shuddering horror that will thrill throughout the world. After this awful picture of the crimes at present committed as it were under the very ægis of the law has been fully unfolded before the eyes of the public, we need not doubt that the House of Commons will find time to raise the age during which English girls are protected from inexpiable wrong. The evidence which we shall publish this week leaves no room for doubt—first, as to the reality of the crimes against which the Amendment Bill is directed, and, secondly, as to the efficacy of the protection extended by raising the age of consent. When the report is published, the case for the bill will be complete, and we do not believe that members on the eve of a general election will refuse to consider the bill protecting the daughters of the poor, which even the House of Lords has in three consecutive years declared to be imperatively necessary.

This, however, is but one, and that one of the smallest, of the considerations which justify the publication of the Report. The good it will do is manifest. These revelations, which we begin to publish to-day, cannot fail to touch the heart and rouse the conscience of the English people. Terrible as is the exposure, the very horror of it is an inspiration. It speaks not of leaden despair, but with a joyful promise of better things to come. *Wir heissen euch hoffen!* "We bid you be of hope," CARLYLE'S last message to his country, the rhythmic word with which GOETHE closes his modern psalm—that is what we have to repeat to-day, for assuredly these horrors, like others against which the conscience of mankind has revolted, are not eternal. "Am I my sister's keeper?" that paraphrase of the excuse of CAIN, will not dull the fierce smart of pain which will be felt by every decent man who learns the kind of atrocities which are being perpetrated in cool blood in the very shadow of our churches and within a stone's throw of our courts. It is a veritable slave trade that is going on around us; but, as it takes place in the heart of London, it is a scandal—an outrage on public morality—even to allude to it. We have kept silence far too long. There are a few devoted workers who have been labouring for years endeavouring to save those who might well address GORDON'S homely reproach to the "majority of us: "While you are eating and drinking and "resting on good beds, we, and those with me, are watching by night and by day"—working against this great wrong—happy, indeed, if they escaped obloquy and abuse for endeavouring to remind us of our duty. No longer will good men be able with easy conscience to join in that indignant "Hush!" by which the evildoers have hitherto silenced every attempt to make articulate the smothered wail that rises unceasing from the woeful under-world. There is now an end to that conspiracy of silence by which, after every inquiry, "the door was each time quickly closed upon "the question, as the stone lid used to be shut down, in the "Campo Santo of Naples, upon the mass of human corpses that "lay festering beneath." That "stone lid" is raised now, never again, we may hope, to be closed until something has been done. Under the ruthless compulsion of publicity even those but indifferent honest will do more good than many of the most virtuous when the evil could be hidden out of sight.

That much may be done, we have good ground for hoping, if only because so little has hitherto been attempted. A dull despair has unnerved the hearts of those who face this monstrous evil, and good men have sorrowfully turned to other fields where their exertions might expect a better return. But the magnitude of this misery ought to lead to the redoubling, not to the benumbing of our exertions. No one can say how much suffering and wrong is irredeemable until the whole of the moral and religious forces of the country are brought to bear upon it. Yet, in dealing with this subject, the forces upon which we rely in dealing with other evils are almost all paralysed. The Home, the School, the Church, the Press are silent. The law is actually accessory to crime. Parents culpably neglect even to warn their children of the existence of dangers of which many learn the first time when they have become their prey. The Press, which reports verbatim all the scabrous details of the divorce courts, recoils in pious horror from the duty of shedding a flood of light upon these dark places, which indeed are full of the habitations of cruelty. But the failure of the

Churches is, perhaps, the most conspicuous and the most complete. CHRIST'S mission was to restore man to a semblance of the Divine. The Child-Prostitute of our day is the image into which, with the tacit acquiescence of those who call themselves by His name, men have moulded the form once fashioned in the likeness of GOD.

If Chivalry is extinct and Christianity is effete, there is still another great enthusiasm to which we may with confidence appeal. The future belongs to the combined forces of Democracy and Socialism, which when united are irresistible. Divided on many points they will combine in protesting against the continued immolation of the daughters of the people as a sacrifice to the vices of the rich. Of the two, it is Socialism which will find the most powerful stimulus in this revelation of the extent to which under our present social system the wealthy are able to exercise all the worst abuses of power which disgraced the feudalism of the Middle Ages. Wealth is power, Poverty is weakness. The abuse of power leads directly to its destruction, and in all the annals of crime can there be found a more shameful abuse of the power of wealth than that by which in this nineteenth century of Christian civilization princes and dukes, and ministers and judges, and the rich of all classes, are purchasing for damnation, temporal if not eternal, the as yet uncorrupted daughters of the poor? It will be said their assent to their corruption. So did the female serfs from whom the seigneur exacted the *jus primæ noctis.* And do our wealthy think that the assent wrung by wealth from poverty to its own undoing will avert the vengeance and the doom?

If people can only be got to think seriously about this matter progress will be made in the right direction. Evils once as universal and apparently inevitable as prostitution have disappeared. Vices almost universal are now regarded with shuddering horror by the least moral of men. Slavery has gone. A slave trader is treated as *hostis humani generis.* Piracy has disappeared. Intestine war is now almost unknown. Torture has been abolished. May we not hope, therefore, that if we try to do our duty to our sisters and to ourselves, we may greatly reduce, even although we never entirely extirpate, the plague of prostitution? For let us remember that—

> Every hope which rises and grows broad
> In the world's heart, by ordered impulse streams
> From the great heart of GOD.

And if that ideal seems too blinding bright for human eyes, we can at least do much to save the innocent victims who unwillingly are swept into the maelstrom of vice. And who is there among us bearing the name of man who will dare to sit down any longer with folded hands in the presence of so great a wrong?

THE MAIDEN TRIBUTE OF MODERN BABYLON.—I.

THE REPORT OF OUR SECRET COMMISSION.

IN ancient times, if we may believe the myths of Hellas, Athens, after a disastrous campaign, was compelled by her conqueror to send once every nine years a tribute to Crete of seven youths and seven maidens. The doomed fourteen, who were selected by lot amid the lamentations of the citizens, returned no more. The vessel that bore them to Crete unfurled black sails as the symbol of despair, and on arrival her passengers were flung into the famous Labyrinth of Dædalus, there to wander about blindly until such time as they were devoured by the Minotaur, a frightful monster, half man, half bull, the foul product of an unnatural lust. "The "labyrinth was as large as a town and had countless courts and galleries. "Those who entered it could never find their way out again. If they "hurried from one to another of the numberless rooms looking for "the entrance door, it was all in vain. They only became more hopelessly "lost in the bewildering labyrinth, until at last they were devoured by "the Minotaur." Twice at each ninth year the Athenians paid the maiden tribute to King Minos, lamenting sorely the dire necessity of bowing to his iron law. When the third tribute came to be exacted, the distress of the city of the Violet Crown was insupportable. From the King's palace to the peasant's hamlet, everywhere were heard cries and groans and the choking sob of despair, until the whole air seemed to vibrate with the sorrow of an unutterable anguish. Then it was that the hero Theseus volunteered to be offered up among those who drew the black balls from the brazen urn of destiny, and the story of his self-sacrifice, his victory, and his triumphant return, is among the most familiar of the tales which since the childhood of the world have kindled

From the streets of London to the corridors of power ... the start of Stead's sensational 'Maiden Tribute' series on child prostitution, for which he purchased a 13-year-old girl for £5.

wealth and public squalor', as we would say today. He wanted 'to use the press to remove the injustices which exist beneath the fair foundations of ... wealth and commerce in Britain'.[46] In other words, his only business was the business of investigative journalism. He was in one of the most influential seats in the country, and it was his job to supply his readers with some worthwhile, functional information, not with mere candyfloss. He was not prepared to play the role of the traditional London editor, offering petty official secrets and society gossip as inducements to those reluctant to pay good money for more and more advertisements. 'The editor,' he proclaimed, 'is the uncrowned king of an educated democracy.' Traditional, deferential journalism was no longer enough. The people had a right to know what was being done in their name by their so-called representatives.[47] Stead was proud of himself as a muckraker for God. But he refused absolutely to be a journalistic moonraker for the *Police News*.[48]

At the age of 15, Stead was inspired by his reading of James Russell Lowell's preface to the 'Pious Editor's Creed': 'What a pulpit the editor mounts daily, sometimes with a congregation of fifty thousand. And from what a Bible he can choose his text, the open volume of the world! Methinks the editor who should understand his calling and be equal thereto, would be the very Moses of our nineteenth century ... the Captain of our Exodus into the Canaan of a truer social order.'[49] A few years later, aged 22, never having seen the inside of a newspaper office, Stead was appointed editor of the *Northern Echo*, published at Darlington and having a circulation of 13,000. And from that moment he became the noisiest journalistic evangelist in the whole of England. He was determined (as he told Mme Novikov) 'to secure the final overthrow of the Powers of Darkness in high places'.[50] In his diary he congratulated himself on the success of his first editorial campaign to prevent Great Britain from becoming embroiled in a war with Russia. He would not, he said, expend many words on 'such immodesty and such self-regard'. But he concluded his entry as follows: 'I have received the highest compliments from Mr Gladstone.' Thus did the young W. T. Stead record his first major step along the road to future notoriety as a campaigning journalist.[51]

Stead as a proud convict at Holloway Gaol, just after the 'Maiden Tribute' trial.

Today it seems incredible that a daily paper that had such a tiny circulation could even pay its way. That its young editor could also think of himself as a partner with the leader of the opposition in shaping Britain's foreign policy is still less easy to credit. There were, of course, no national newspapers in 1877, in the sense in which we define them today. Indeed, according to Gladstone himself, there was more political power in the provincial press in 'this year of crisis for *The Times*' than in the whole of the London press.[52] As late as 1882, Joseph Hatton, the Conservative editor of the *People*, remarked that 'it is provincial England, not journalistic London, that makes and unmakes Parliament'.[53] But Gladstone's remark was made after he had already invited the young fire-eater to assist John Morley at the *Pall Mall Gazette*. There was as yet no recognition of the news function as the primary purpose of the newspaper. A 'viewspaper' was all that was required. But there was belated recognition of young Stead's point that the Liberal party press in Fleet Street as well as in the provinces should become 'the engine of social reform'.[54] It is therefore no exaggeration to say that Stead's journalistic efforts were motivated as much by what he passionately believed were urgent political needs as they were by his religious and social obsessions. Perhaps one of the best illustrations of this powerful mixture occurs in a sad little tale told by Annie Besant just after his death in 1912: 'If Stead's championship of the unemployed alienated the clubmen of Pall Mall, that only made it the more reason why he and I should trudge on foot together, from Soho to Mile End, beside the body of the workless man struck down on Trafalgar Square on Bloody Sunday.'[55]

Stead's greatest personal theme, however, was the unlimited range of a free journalist's powers and responsibilities. The divine right of kings had gone, Stead argued; so too had the divine right of the gentry entrenched in Parliament, the Church, the universities, and the land. It was now being challenged by the divine right of demagogues to speak for the people in the language of the people. The free press was impatiently taking over the function of the Commons. (Stead informed the Prince of Wales during an extended and exclusive press interview that he would on no account exchange places with him!) A newspaper, he declared, must 'palpitate with actuality'; it must be a mirror reflecting all the currents and phases of life in the locality. The press, he affirmed, 'has become to the Commons what the Commons once were to the Lords. The Press has become the Chamber of Initiative and this new power of initiation it has secured by natural right.'[56]

All this, of course, could have been dismissed as windy rhetoric except for three facts. First, Stead always practised what he preached. He went always for the primary sources of information and treated official news sources with great suspicion. Second, he was remarkably successful at raising money for good causes and arranging practical help for people in trouble – especially legal trouble. Third, his plan to enable the press to exercise legitimate civil power through a national network of unpaid volunteers, similar to the unpaid JP system which had networked the country for two centuries outside London, was not merely radically democratic; it was also perfectly feasible given the sort of official cooperation that he had in mind. He proposed that each newspaper should have its own whip in Parliament, should be invested with the right to inspect all official institutions, and should be assisted by press agents in each government department. 'The duty of an editor,' he declared, 'is absolute. He ought to be able to get at, or know someone who can get at, everyone from the Queen downwards, in order to be able to ascertain what they are thinking about the topic of the day.' He should be 'universally accessible', know everyone and hear everything. According to Stead,

> The old-fashioned idea of a jealously shrouded impersonality has given way to its exact antithesis. There is something inexpressibly pathetic in the dumbness of the masses of the people. Touch but a hair on the head of the well-to-do and forthwith, you will hear his protest in the august columns of *The Times*. But the millions who have to suffer the rudest buffets of ill-fortune, those victims of official insolence and the brutality of the better-off, they are as dumb as the HORSE, which you may scourge to death without its uttering a sound... To give utterance to the inarticulate moan of the voiceless, is to let some light into a dark place; it is almost equivalent to the enfranchisement of a class... To be both eye and ear for the community is a great privilege. However, power no less than noblesse, obliges – and much may be done to realize it if we but recognize that the discharge of such responsibility lies in the day's work of every journalist.[57]

Yes, it was a fine piece of oratorical writing. It was also an innovative idea – one that might easily have turned the Fleet Street press into a fourth branch of government. But it got him into immediate trouble with the Establishment. It was too radical by half. And not even Harold Evans, his twentieth-century counterpart in both Darlington and London,[58] would be able to turn it into a practical reality 70 years later. Both men eventually had to take themselves off to America where they spiritually and mentally belonged.[59]

But, to return to Stead's emotional cadenza, it may have brought him trouble with his political bosses, but it also brought him to the brink of his most creative journalistic idea: the *endowed* newspaper. This is how Stead, writing in 1886, introduced the concept:

> If some great newspaper proprietor will not content himself with only a reasonable fortune – and will not agree to devote the surplus of his gigantic profits to turning his newspaper into an engine of social reform and a means of government – well then, perhaps some man or woman of fortune will be prepared to devote a mere half-million to *endow* a newspaper, free of all advertising, for the service, for the education and for the guidance of the people?

He then outlined the steps necessary to 'gauge, and at the same time influence', the opinion of the nation. Mere circulation, he insisted, would not avail. Influence depends not half so much on quantity as upon the quality of the subscribers. How then? 'There are two methods: the first is by a system of major-generals, and the second by a system of journalistic travellers.'

He began with the system of major-generals. 'When Cromwell was driven to undertake the governing of England, he mapped out the towns into districts, and over each district he placed a man after his own heart, responsible to him for the peace and good government of the district under his care.' That system, Stead declared, could be adopted with advantage by any newspaper that wished to keep in hand the affairs of the whole country:

> A competent, intelligent, sympathetic man or woman, as nearly as possible the *alter ego* of the editor, should be planted in each district and held responsible for keeping the editor informed of all that is going on within the area that needs attending to, either for encouragement or repression, or merely for observation and report... It would also be the duty of the major-general to select one associate who would undertake to co-operate with the central office in ascertaining facts, in focussing opinion, and in generally assisting the editor to ascertain the direct views of his countrymen... It might be a squire or it might be a cobbler; it might be the clergyman's daughter, or a secularist newsagent, or a Methodist reporter... And to each there will be posted copies of the paper, in recognition of their position and services, and in order to keep them in touch with the editorial mind.

Each of the major-generals would exercise general oversight over all the associates in his division, but the whole organization would be kept together and the personal sense of a common interest kept up 'by the periodical visits of the journalistic traveller...' These 'peripatetic apostles of the New Journalism' would, he thought, bring the whole organization alive and instil a common interest and a common enthusiasm. If all this was done, the newspaper would become the most powerful and one of the most useful institutions in the country:

> Such a newspaper would indeed be a great secular or civic church and democratic university, and if wisely directed and energetically worked, it would come to be the very soul of our national

unity; and its great central idea would be that of the self-sacrifice of the individual for the salvation of the community, the practical realization of the religious idea in national politics and social reform.

Parliament, he concluded, has reached its utmost development.

> There is now need of a new representative method, not to supersede but to supplement that which exists – a system which will be more elastic, more simple, more direct and more closely in touch with the mind of the people… And when the time does arrive, and the man and the money are both forthcoming, government by journalism will no longer be a somewhat hyperbolical phrase, but a solid fact.[60]

Well, as we know, nothing happened along these lines – at least not during Stead's lifetime – apart from an abortive effort by Stead to produce a newspaper called the *Daily Paper*, which started in 1904 and lasted only three weeks. The world première of the endowed newspaper was delayed until 1940 when Ralph Ingersoll launched an adless newspaper in New York, *PM*, which lasted in various forms until 1948.[61] What a pity it now seems that Stead did not find it in himself to accept Cecil Rhodes's offer to buy him the *Fall Mall Gazette* or 'some other paper to experiment with'.[62] If he had, it might have given Great Britain a much more businesslike precedent than *PM* for the totally adless, endowed newspaper.

We know that throughout the years 1890–3 Stead was daydreaming continually of the wonderful and unique daily paper that he would soon produce. Unfortunately, not even his well-publicized trip to Chicago in 1893 brought him any closer to his elusive 'millionaire with vision'. Part of the trouble was self-doubt. 'I do not think that money is the difficulty at all,' he is quoted as saying just before he left for Chicago, 'the difficulty lies not in the Capitalist but in the Editor. I am a bad manager. I am a very good Master when I have a very good Servant, but I am a very bad Master, indeed the worst, when I have a bad Servant because I am not hard enough to keep him up to his work.'[63] In other words, like most egomaniacs, he was quite unable to delegate responsibility, preferring to do everything himself even when he was clearly not up to it! All his doubts about himself, however, had gone, and he was back to his usual, ebullient self by the time of his interview with the Chicago *Sunday Tribune* on 10 November 1893. The interview begins abruptly:

> 'If ever there was a demagogue,' said William T. Stead, the London editor, as he slipped further down into his chair and propped his feet up on the railing, 'if ever there was a demagogue in the world, I am one. I'd rather be a demagogue any day, than a Brahmin! It is only necessary that the demagogue should be moved by right ideas.'

This is only the opening paragraph of an hilarious interview. Stead continued:

> One of the things I looked forward to in coming to Chicago was meeting your late Mayor, Carter Harrison. He has been called a demagogue. He had, I am told, a premonition of his violent taking off. I have had a similar warning. I am to die a violent death also, but, before death comes to me, I am to be twice more locked up in prison for my journalism.

The interviewer then asked him whether there was anything about the American newspapers he particularly disliked.

'Yes, there are,' Stead replied, 'Many. Above all, the way in which American proprietors of newspapers sell their souls to the advertiser, showing no other ambition than to heap up an immense fortune and fatten on their gains. They have not even as much public spirit as the medieval robber barons.'

What did he mean by that, asked the man from the *Tribune*:

'Well, what I mean is this: in the old days when a man had made his pile, he used it to govern and civilize and educate the people in the midst of whom he had established his castle. But there is no such recognition of responsibility on the part of most newspaper proprietors nowadays.

'Instead of regarding the wealth they have acquired as merely the starting point for humanizing the conditions of life among those whose support has provided their wealth, they live self-indulgent, self-centered lives. As individuals they may be excellent persons, but from the point of view of the social organization they are but the fatted swine of civilization.'

Stead was then asked whether it was possible to change the system. His reply was: 'Yes. But it can be changed only by bringing back into existence the real live

Popular support for Stead outside the Northumberland Street office of the *Pall Mall Gazette*, vehicle for his 'Maiden Tribute' series and other 'escapades'.

Church... We need to use the newspaper as a social pillory in which those who have received much and returned nothing to the community will be stigmatized as they deserve.' The *Tribune* man asked: 'Was it business?' 'Yes, of course – the very best business,' Stead replied warmly, 'Read all about THE MIRACLE WORKER OF NAZARETH in this Sunday's paper – That's good business too! So let's have no more of this cheap cynicism!'[64]

Thus spoke 'God's Englishman' – managing to sound more like Jehovah than even his model, Oliver Cromwell, was wont to do! He then launched into further morals of thunder against another of his journalistic *bêtes noires*, the night editor! Stead's main conception of an editor's duty, without a doubt, was to be like himself. He had come to the realization, as no editor before him had done, not even Barnes or Delane of *The Times*, what power a newspaper could give him to record himself with headlines and bold type, with recitative and chorus, on a pedestal of fact and news once in every 24 hours. Stead's mercurial, hellfire temperament was that of the great pamphleteers. In his boldness and versatility, in his passionate belief in the constructive power of the pen, in so many of his opinions, even in his championship of women, he resembled Daniel Defoe and Jonathan Swift.

He was also a great popularizer, a great translator of the deliberately obscure language of the specialist in terms that most busy generalists could enjoy as well as understand. But his great, almost mesmeric, power over men's minds had its deepest root in the Christian sincerity that every page of his writing confessed. Even by Victorian standards, he was outstanding here. Mr Gladstone, his most famous guide and mentor, sounded worldly by comparison, and the range of his devotees extended from Cardinal Manning to Annie Besant.

John Ruskin was by no means the only master of letters ready to overlook Stead's journalese in appreciation of his flair for drawing public attention to great moral and political purposes. George Bernard Shaw, a great destroyer of false idols, also felt this way. Here are a few sentences from the very long letters they both wrote to the *Pall Mall Gazette* in June 1887. First, Ruskin:

> Permit me to advise you that the function of the P.M.G. is neither to teach theology nor to criticize art. You have taken an honest and powerful position in modern politics and ethics, and you have nothing whatever to do with traditions of eternal punishment, but only to bring, so far as you may know, immediate malefactors to immediate punishment.

Now, Shaw:

> Sir, your paper enjoys a peculiar opportunity – that of leader of the Press in the march to meet the coming twentieth century. Your rivals are too blind, too deaf, too dumb and too full of notions of literary propriety – which are misplaced frivolities. The P.M.G. owes its unique position wholly to its memorable resolution to attack social abuses with the terrible weapon of truth-telling. If you sheath that weapon, what will maintain that paper in its present place when the Afghan frontier and Home Rule are forgotten? I venture to predict that the future is with journals like the Gazette, which will dare to tell polite society that it lives by the robbery and murder of the poor, and will ask pardon of the poor for its tacit approval of such robbery and murder in the past.[65]

Ruskin and Shaw were hard-headed men who had been around London's club-land, where the establishment resided, much longer than Stead. Their praise was not given lightly. They plainly wanted him to succeed and to persist, despite all the forces ranged against him. They recognized that, although no contemporary editor had worked harder at self-education or knew more persons of mark in high society, Stead's upbringing and adult life were, in some respects, narrow. For example, as Robertson Scott, Stead's biographer, tells us, it was not until some years after Stead left the *Pall Mall Gazette* that he paid his first visit to the theatre! They also saw that Stead was emotionally immature, like so many self-made intellectuals. He was frequently referred to in public as childlike. Nevertheless, he was able to secure excellent interviews with the Tsar of all the Russias as well as with the Prince of Wales, and his 'Letters from the Vatican', published serially in October and November 1889, added considerably to his world reputation at the time.

His political radicalism seems to reach back to Cromwell and Lilburne and the Puritan Revolution. It was right out of its time, being almost pure 'Mayflower' or mid-Atlantic in spirit. Stead's ideological focus helped to remove academic doubts about the continuing existence of an Anglo-American journalistic tradition of dissent.[67] Stead, in his buttoned-up English way, was consciously trying to imitate Horace Greeley of the *New York Tribune*.[68] He was not at all concerned with emulating that arch exploiter of the American public, James Gordon Bennett of the *New York Herald*. But then he was not desirous of emigrating and becoming an American either – which is why I have suggested that he is somewhat mid-Atlantic in spirit and therefore alienated from both worlds. It is frustrating, for us as well as for him, that he never became an adequately financed newspaper owner in either country. He could have shown the world what he would have done with an endowed newspaper, if he had been in sole charge of one.

He managed one thing very well indeed, while still at the height of his powers in the 1880s before he became involved with his 'spooks' and 'that dreadful craze of his about departed spirits'.[69] He provided a salutary reminder to all governments that, in the words of a seventeenth-century poet,

There is on earth a yet Auguster thing,
  Veiled though it be than Parliament and King

namely, democracy or government by journalism. This reminder was noted carefully at the time on both sides of the Atlantic, though more especially on the New York side, where his political views seemed more naturally to belong. When Stead died in 1912, the *New York Sun* expressed the view, in all seriousness, that 'in the years between 1884 and 1888, Stead came nearer to governing Great Britain than any other man in the kingdom'.[70] Stead's 'shade' would have liked that! Mr Gladstone and, of course, Lord Esher would have demurred. But not many others among his contemporaries, even in Great Britain, would have wished to do likewise.

7 'A Street of Hasty Judgement and Elastic Morality'

(John Francis Gore, 1928)

'By 1914', according to historian G. M. Trevelyan, 'the Philistines had captured the Ark of the Covenant and learnt how to work their own miracles through its power'. Northcliffe was now 'making marvels out of nothing' and several other 'unprincipled grocers', it was felt, were 'selling news like soap'. The newspaper was no longer even remotely 'a civilizing force' and, according to Gore (upset by the 'incredible' divorce court reporting that was then permitted), Fleet Street had become 'a street of hasty judgement, of distorted truth, of elastic morality, of easy conviction'. The Street of Adventure was rapidly transforming itself into a street of shame.

By the end of the century, Reuters messengers were a familiar sight in the City.

Above 'Waiting for *Lloyd's Newspaper*', a popular skit of B. R. Haydon's familiar coffee-house scene 'Waiting for *The Times*'.

Above Left   Karl Marx (1818–83), portrayed here by Gerald Scarfe as a brooding prophet diverting the river of history, never claimed to be anything but a journalist. When forced to leave his native Germany in 1849, he became London correspondent (1851–62) for the *New York Daily Tribune*, based in Fleet Street, being helped with his English by his Manchester businessman friend, Friedrich Engels. (Cover drawing for the 1983 edition of *Journalism Studies Review*)

Above Right   Edward Lloyd (1815–90) has been described as the most successful proprietor in Fleet Street newspaper history before Alfred Harmsworth. The repeal of the Stamp Act and the purchase of a Hoe press boosted rising sales of his *Lloyd's Weekly Newspaper* – published from Salisbury Square – to a world record of more than 1 million.

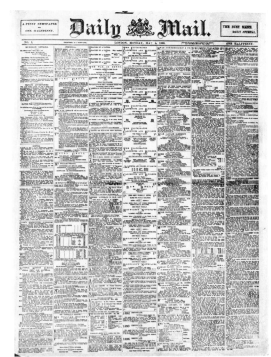

Right *Daily Mail*, No. 1, 4 May 1896 (registration issues had started in February).

Below The chairman's office at Carmelite House, built 1897–9. This witnessed the transformation of plain Mr Harmsworth into all-powerful Viscount Northcliffe.

Above The chairman's office becomes boardroom: this interior has been carefully preserved and re-created in the new offices for the *Daily Mail* and its associates in Northcliffe House, Kensington.

Left Viscount Northcliffe, his brother the 1st Viscount Rothermere and, in the centre, the Hon. Esmond Harmsworth, later 2nd Viscount Rothermere.

Top Left   H. Wickham Steed, editor of *The Times*, lands in the USA with 'the Chief' (Northcliffe), 1921.

Top Right   Philip Gibbs published his classic novel *The Street of Adventure* in 1909, based on his working life with the new *Daily Mail*, *The Daily Chronicle* and *Tribune*. This likeness by Helen Wilson appeared much later in his long career, after he had served throughout the First World War as an official war correspondent and been knighted.

Bottom Left   Thomas Marlowe, editor of the *Daily Mail* from 1899 to 1926, 'rarely presumed to say no', weathering successive storms with 'the Chief' by accepting his status as a hireling.

Bottom Right   J. L. Garvin, *The Observer* personified while it was backed by Northcliffe and later by Waldorf (1st Viscount) Astor, portrayed by Alick Ritchie in *Vanity Fair*, 1911. St Dunstan-in-the-West Church has a memorial plaque to Garvin as well as a bust of Northcliffe on its Fleet Street frontage.

The Daily Telegraph's building at 135 Fleet Street was rebuilt incorporating Peterborough Court and opened with royal patronage in 1882. Like so many newspaper offices, this was set off by an imposing clock. (Photographed in 1913, National Buildings Record)

Right *The Daily Telegraph*'s linotypes in 1913: the paper was forced to buy them in order to keep pace with the *Daily Mail*.

Bottom Left *The Daily Chronicle*, founded in 1869, had a distinctive headquarters in Salisbury Square. Long afterwards, in 1930, *The Daily Chronicle* and the *Daily News* combined under Laurence Cadbury and Walter (later Lord) Layton as the Liberal *News Chronicle*, housed with its evening partner, the *Star*, in Bouverie Street. Both papers ceased overnight in 1960 – an event still greatly mourned.

Bottom Right Will Dyson's uncannily prescient cartoon in the *Daily Herald*, 17 May 1919, following the signing of the Treaty of Versailles. 'The Tiger' was Georges Clemenceau, France's Prime Minister, depicted leading out the Allied delegates.

Opposite The 25th birthday of the *Daily Mail* (4 May 1921), when this first of 16 broadsheet pages featured the leading London stores – among them Barkers, then occupying the building in Kensington where the paper is now produced.

PEACE AND FUTURE CANNON FODDER

The Tiger: "Curious! I seem to hear a child weeping!"

16 LARGE PAGES

Daily Mail

Daily Mail 25TH BIRTHDAY NUMBER

OVER 1,350,000 NET SALE.

LONDON, MANCHESTER, PARIS. NO. 7,820. WEDNESDAY, MAY 4, 1921. ONE PENNY.

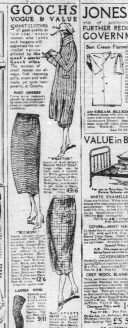
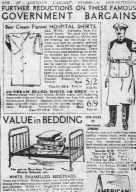

Right Skywriting and a massive sign symbolize the confident *Daily Mail* in this composite 1924 publicity picture. Instigated by Northcliffe, the prizes offered to air pioneers by the newspaper are part of aviation history.

The Times

No. 44263   London Wednesday, May 5, 1926.   Price 2d

WEATHER FORECAST. Wind N.E., fair to dull: risk of rain.

THE GENERAL STRIKE.

A wide response was made yesterday throughout the country to the call of those Unions which had been ordered by the T.U.C. to bring out their members. Railway workers stopped generally, though at Hull railway clerks are reported to have resumed duty, confining themselves to their ordinary work, and protested against the strike. Commercial road transport was only partially suspended. In London the tramways and L.G.O.C. services were stopped. The printing industry is practically at a standstill, but lithographers have not been withdrawn, and compositors in London have not received instructions to strike. Large numbers of building operatives, other than those working on housing, came out.

The situation in the engineering trades was confused; men in some districts stopped while in others they continued at work. There was no interference with new construction in the ship building yards, but in one or two districts some of the men engaged on repair work joined in the strike with the dockers.

Food — Supplies of milk and fish brought into London from Hyde Park and Paddington were successfully distributed from the Milk & Food Controller expects it will be possible to maintain a satisfactory supply of milk to hospitals, institutions, schools, hotels, restaurants and private consumers. Milk will be 8d. per gallon dearer wholesale and 2d. per quart retail today. Smithfield market has distributed 5,000 tons of meat since Monday.

Mails — Efforts will be made to forward by means of road transport the mails already shown as due to be dispatched shortly from London. The position is uncertain and the facilities may have to be limited to mails for America, India and Africa.

At Bow Street Mr. Saklatvala, M.P., who was required as a result of his Hyde Park speech on Saturday to give sureties to abstain from making violent and inflammatory speeches, was remanded for two days on bail.

Full tram and (or) bus services were running yesterday at Bristol, Lincoln, Southampton, Aldershot, Bournemouth and Isle-of-Wight, and partial services in Edinburgh, Glasgow, Liverpool, Leeds, Northampton, Cardiff, Portsmouth, Dover, N.Derbyshire and Monmouthshire.

Evening papers appeared at Bristol, Southampton, several Lancashire towns and Edinburgh, and typescript issues at Manchester, Birmingham and Aberdeen.

The Atlantic Fleet did not sail on its summer cruise from Portsmouth yesterday. The men went on shore duty.

Road and Rail Transport — There was no railway passenger transport in London yesterday except a few suburban trains. Every available form of transport was used. A few independent omnibuses were running, but by the evening the railway companies, except the District and Tubes, had an improvised service.

Among the railway services to-day will be 6.30 a.m. Manchester to Marylebone; 6.30 a.m.Marylebone to Manchester; 10.10 a.m. Marylebone to Newcastle; 9 a.m. Norwich to London; 9 a.m. King's Cross to York; 3 p.m. King's Cross to Peterborough; 9 p.m. Peterborough to King's Cross. L.M.S. Electric trains will maintain a 40 minutes service. On all sections of the Metropolitan Railway except Moorgate to Finsbury Park a good service will run to-day from 6.40 a.m.

The Underground hope to work a six minutes service on the Central London Line today from 8 a.m. to 8 p.m. between Wood Lane and Liverpool Street. The following stations only will be open:— Shepherds Bush, Lancaster Gate, Oxford Circus, Tottenham Court Road, Bank, Liverpool Street. A flat fare of 3d will be charged.

The Prime Minister had an audience of the King yesterday morning.

There was no indication last night of any attempt to resume negotiations between the Prime Minister and the T.U.C.

The Government is printing an official newspaper, "The British Gazette" which will appear today, price 1d. It will be distributed throughout the London area. Volunteers for the London Underground Railways and for L.G.O.C. omnibuses should communicate with the Commercial Manager's Department, 55 Broadway, S.W.

The Prince of Wales returned to London from Biarritz last night travelling from Paris by air.

The British Gazette

PLEASE PASS ON THIS COPY OR DISPLAY IT

Published by His Majesty's Stationery Office.

No. 8   LONDON, THURSDAY, MAY 13, 1926.   ONE PENNY.

GENERAL STRIKE OFF

UNCONDITIONAL WITHDRAWAL OF NOTICES BY T.U.C.

Men To Return Forthwith.

SURRENDER RECEIVED BY PREMIER IN DOWNING STREET.

Negotiations To Be Resumed In The Coal Dispute.

The General Strike, which began at midnight on Monday, May 3, ended yesterday in an unconditional withdrawal of the strike notices by the General Council of the Trades Union Congress. The news of the settlement was conveyed to the public in the following official communiqués:—

WHITEHALL, May 12.

It was intimated to the Prime Minister that the Trades Union Council desired to come and see him at Downing-street, and they arrived soon after 12 noon. Mr. Pugh made a statement, in which he stated that the Trades Union Council had decided to call off the strike notices forthwith.

The Prime Minister then spoke briefly. He stated that he was very glad to hear what Mr. Pugh had said, and he would report it to his colleagues in the Cabinet.

As regards the coal industry, the Prime Minister said that negotiations would be resumed, and the Government would consider to what steps should be taken.

THE KING TO THE NATION

Appeal For Lasting Peace.

MR. BALDWIN ON THE FINISH

Victory Of Common Sense.

STATEMENT IN PARLIAMENT.

THE BIRTH AND LIFE OF THE "BRITISH GAZETTE"

An Unexampled Achievement In Journalism.

HOW AN IMPROVISED NEWSPAPER REACHED A CIRCULATION OF 2,209,000.

"British Gazette" Circulation.

May 5	232,000
May 6	507,000
May 7	655,000
May 8	836,000
May 10	1,022,000
May 11	1,427,000
May 12	**2,209,000**

The Morning Post.

ON FRIDAY, MAY 14

THE MORNING POST

will

RESUME PUBLICATION

Price ONE Penny

Left 'Good Luck in the New Year': *The Graphic*'s optimism for 1926 came unstuck five months later, when the country suffered the General Strike and Fleet Street was reduced to 'miserable sheets'.

Opposite Left *The Times*, No. 44263, 5 May 1926 (the second day of the nine-day General Strike). has since become famous as the 'Little Sister' issue.

Opposite Right On 13 May 1926 *The British Gazette*, the official makeshift newspaper edited by Winston Churchill, proudly announced the end of the General Strike.

Max , Lord Beaverbrook.

Opposite Top Left   Max Aitken, 1st Baron Beaverbrook. His first Fleet Street venture was to secure control of the *Daily Express* in 1916. He then launched the *Sunday Express* in 1918 and finally acquired the controlling interest in the *Evening Standard* in 1923.

Opposite Top Right   Remarkably, David Low was allowed to caricature his long-time employer, Beaverbrook, with impunity. This was a measure of both his skill and his unique standing.

Opposite Bottom   Beaverbrook felt that he needed a consummate technician to edit the *Daily Express* and in Arthur Christiansen he found his man. Here Christiansen acts himself in the 1962 film *The Day the Earth Caught Fire*. He died the following year, a broken man, at the age of 59.

Above   The original Northcliffe House (at the junction of Tudor Street and Bouverie Street) was opened by the Prince of Wales (later Edward VIII) in May 1927. Rothermere is on his right and the Hon. Esmond Harmsworth is in the group on his left.

The *Daily Express* (1933), with black vitrolite and glass covering for its concrete frame, made every other Fleet Street building look staid. But the classic lines of the rebuilt *Daily Telegraph* alongside remained in keeping with its own 'quality' stance. Interestingly, Sir Owen Williams was consulting engineer for both.

Above Left   The *Daily Express* sub-editors' room (*c.*1933) was much more prosaic.

Above Right   Hannen Swaffer learnt his trade on Northcliffe's *Daily Mail* in the early days of the century, and characterfully adorned six other national newspapers. As Tom Driberg, his biographer, records: 'Any day in the 1930s, 1940s or 1950s a tall, cadaverous, elderly man could be seen strolling, or rather stalking meditatively... His antiquated black clothes, a floppy black tie or stock, a black hat as rusty as the rest of his gear, a fag-end, nearly finished, drooping from his mouth...'

Left   Low, knighted in 1962 mainly because of his insight and wit but also because of his artistry, had by then become undisputed king of political cartoonists.

Above Carmelite House, still the hub of *Daily Mail* production in 1936, had been supplemented by the construction of New Carmelite House beyond. The *Evening News* was its sister paper until 1980.

Right The plaque to Edgar Wallace in Ludgate Circus reminds us that, after being a paperboy on that very spot, his career led via journalism and novels galore to glitzy Hollywood film studios (as here). Wallace first found his astonishing dexterity with words in the South African War, serving Reuters and the *Daily Mail*, returning to be their crime correspondent in the first of a string of Fleet Street jobs.

Above Right   The chairman's office on the sumptuous fifth floor of the *Daily Telegraph* building. In the place of honour is a portrait of William Berry, 1st Viscount Camrose, whose office this was from 1928 to 1954. In his successful career, marked by a memorial in St Paul's Cathedral crypt, he was also editor-in-chief of *The Sunday Times* for 22 years (1915–37) and of *The Financial Times* for 24 (1921–45).

Above Left   Gomer Berry, 1st Viscount Kemsley, younger brother of Camrose, whose partner he was for most of his life. In 1937 he took over on his own account the *Daily Sketch*, *The Sunday Times*, three other nationally distributed Sundays, and the provincial chain later renamed Kemsley Newspapers.

Left   A rare shot of the publicity-shy – but highly effective – Sir Emsley Carr, installed as editor-in-chief of the *News of the World* in 1891 and still in office at the time of his death 50 years later. The circulation of the paper was then approaching 8 million every Sunday.

131

8   The Living Legacy

Fleet Street began as a royal highway to the City – and ended, according to Lord Deedes, as 'a Royal nightmare for the newspaper industry'. (He was not, of course, referring solely to *The Sun*.) When it began is best left to the archaeologists: when it ended is a matter, perhaps, for the Darwinists and Monetarists, although Marxists have a lot to say on the subject and may well get the last word, if and when the new 'Wall-Street-in-Europe' goes bust. But, whatever the outcome, the Fleet Street 'angle' will never die – it is immortal, like Max Miller, 'the Cheekie Chappie', or *Citizen Kane*, the film of a legend.

Most people (when they think about the subject at all) tend to think like Lord Deedes, about a 'merciful release' or diaspora, which began in January 1986 with the removal by Rupert Murdoch of four nationals to Wapping, ending in March 1989 with the delayed departure of the *Daily Express* and *Sunday Express* to the other side of Blackfriars Bridge. Such people would benefit from a closer reading of Jewish history: when the Jews were *forced* out of the Holy Land at the time of the destruction of the Temple (586 BC), there was no compensation. The national exodus from Fleet Street, however, produced a £1 billion windfall for the owners of Britain's biggest daily titles. Sales of the buildings, dating from the 1890s (with a few additions built in the 1930s), netted each of today's press barons millions of pounds of sheer profit. And when that old carrier pigeon news co-operative, Reuters, went public, 'it was like finding oil in your back garden', according to one highly-placed Fleet Street executive.

Most of those who *do* read history, like James Curran, try to bring an informed nostalgia to the subject rather than unbounded cynicism. They look back to the so-called 'Golden Age' when a more public-spirited paternalism ruled in Fleet Street. They, like Curran, seem to prefer the mutation theory above any other: that a sudden, shocking change in the gene, or unit of hereditary material known as 'a free press', resulted in an entirely new inheritable characteristic. Whether there has ever been, or ever will be 'a free press', we need not go into here, but this is what he says on mutation: 'The capitalist development of the press (in 1855) encouraged the absorption or elimination of the early radical press and effectively stifled its re-emergence.'[71]

In other words, Dissent died when de-regulation began and never emerged again? If this were true, there would be very little in Fleet Street's history worth celebrating. It is a challenging thought, but far too simplistic. Market forces were at work in Fleet Street from its earliest days as a news centre. They did not appear suddenly in 1855. Nor did they 'finally triumph over radicalism' in the 1890s, nor even in the 1980s. They are an integral part of the news business and will remain so wherever and however news is made. Dissent, too, is alive and well, living somewhere in obscurity and making occasional appearances on television – like Salman Rushdie. It is probably the most indestructible element in the Fleet Street 'outlook' adopted by the Fifth Estate – Broadcasting: the living legacy we can all learn from when the dust dies down and the plaques are replaced.

For most of the past 500 years, Fleet Street was little more than an appendage of the City of London. It is this once more. It was also a raffish, no-man's land between imperial London and provincial London, where money was a subject for analysis, and literary discourse rather more than a quick chat. Even this is still discernible, if only in the faces of its inhabitants and the ruins of old buildings. But its continuing interest in money news was not always uppermost in its mind or even in its output. For a brief moment, historically speaking, its 'general will' was distracted by completely different ideas stemming from the French Revolution and the rise of the Romantic movement.

These two 'adventures in humanism', born of a desire to drive wedges into the smooth surface of ordered society in a most violent manner, transformed Fleet Street totally. They are crucial to any understanding of its subsequent history and the source of most of the political myths. From 1789 until the collapse of the Liberal Party in the 1890s, Fleet Street was a national theatre for Dissent like never before or since. It was 'a babel of competitive roarings', a 'focus of vulgarity and sedition', and 'a republican stronghold' urging 'Revolution by correspondence'. Issues had emerged which people, especially urban people, felt passionately about – political, social and economic. Urban life was hard and rough, and the vast majority of the new reading public did not want to be 'instructed'. They wanted what their friend, William Cobbett, told them they wanted: 'an improvement in our condition', and if that was not possible immediately, they wanted to emigrate. 'For those Atlantic REPUBLICANS have shown us that men can eat, and drink, and sleep, and have children and homes and firesides and trade . . . and yet have NO NATIONAL DEBT and NO KING' (*Poor Man's Guardian*, 22 October 1831).

But it was not simply the radical press which was able to reproduce these feelings and achieve bigger and bigger circulations, especially on Sundays. The 'respectable' press also believed that, to survive and thrive, it must take its 'representative' place in political society, and must cease to be regarded as either a pariah or a dangerous demagogue. It must occupy some kind of middle ground, between 'physical force' revolution on the one hand and 'mealy-mouthed' subservience on the other. With its head in politics and its feet in commerce, it would

G. W. M. Reynolds, a lawyer for the Chartist Movement, made a small fortune out of popular journalism in mid-Victorian times. He founded *Reynolds's Weekly Newspaper* in 1850; the name survived (as *Reynolds News*) until 1962.

soon show the world that the 'Fourth Estate' idea was much more than a myth – it was a mandatory statement.

According to Delane's famous *Times* leader of February 1852:

> The press is daily and for ever appealing to the enlightened force of public opinion – anticipating, if possible, the march of events – standing upon the reach between the present and the future, and extending its survey to the horizon of the world.

It was a grandiose claim, and one that almost deserved the sarcasm it received from beleaguered Tories. 'Who has not heard of Mount Olympus [Anthony Trollope demanded in 1855] – that high abode of all the powers of type... that wondrous habitation of gods and devils, from whence issue forth fifty thousand nightly edicts for the governance of a subject nation?' Disgusted 'Citizens' like Bronterre O'Brien, editor of the *Southern Star*, alleged that Mount Olympus and its pope could be bought for gold. Nevertheless, the pope under review was never wrong, ever vigilant and remarkably all-knowing. 'From the palaces of St. Petersburg to the cabins of Connaught, nothing can escape him.'[72]

For those without any political inclination, or even the courage to emigrate, G. W. M. Reynolds, 'professional democrat' and 'a political humbug all round', had the answer: stay home, stay sober, and 'improve' yourself on Sundays. On his death in 1899, *The Bookseller* declared that 'Dickens, Thackeray and Lever had their thousands of readers, but Mr Reynolds's readers were numbered by hundreds of thousands, perhaps by millions'. *Reynolds's Weekly News* (founded in 1850), Edward Lloyd's *Weekly News* (founded in 1842), the *News of the World* (1843) and the *Weekly Times* (1847) – all 'improving' Sunday newspapers – all reached the million-mark long before the new mass press existed, achieving it with that well-tried Fleet Street formula: sex, crime and radical politics.

Another pope, W. T. Stead, arose in the 1880s, as we have seen, making even more grandiose claims for the 'Fourth Estate' and 'Government by Journalism'. He could not be put down by ostracism or even by imprisonment, largely because he was governed by a series of premonitions or 'signposts' supplied by his 'Senior Partner', as he called God. It also helped that he had a powerful friend in Lord Esher, sharing access to the primary sources of functional information, particularly the secret Treasury accounts. Unfortunately, for the last 20 years of his life, Stead became obsessed by the world of what he jovially called 'spooks'.

He discovered that he possessed the occult power of automatic writing and cheerfully took dictation from the spirits of Mr Gladstone, Lord Tennyson and Catherine the Great. By this time, Stead was impervious to criticism of any kind. His 'spooks' had an easier time getting through to him than did his Fleet Street contemporaries, Frederick Greenwood and A. G. Gardiner, whose fearful warnings about 'hubris' were echoed more recently by Charles Wintour, former editor of the *Evening Standard,* writing in 1988:

> *Government* by journalism is a myth. Sometimes newspapers and television can destroy a man's reputation, but that is not government. Sometimes they can cast light on dark corners – corruption, carelessness, neglect, bureaucratic bungling, social evils, etc – that is not government either, although it helps government. Government means exercising real authority over the key political questions of the day, such as the level of taxation, how the safety of the state is to be secured, what provision should be made for the 'under-privileged'. Journalism, at its best, may highlight areas that need attention but it does not take the decisions, and to claim too much for it can alienate the readers without whom the best editors and the best journalists are powerless.[73]

This is all too true. And Stead, in his early days, would probably have agreed, 'up to a point, Lord Copper'. Nevertheless, Stead and, following in his footsteps, T. P. O'Connor, editor of London's evening *Star* from 1888, did much to humanize as well as revolutionize journalism in Britain. Before their day, the respectable press had conceded little to human feeling. The *Pall Mall Gazette* and the *Star*, on the other hand, touched life in all its parts in a manner that was 'radiant, radical and

This bust of T. P. O'Connor (1848–1929) of the *Star*, London's first 'new journalism' evening paper, appears on Chronicle House, 72 Fleet Street, and carries the legend: 'His pen could lay bare the bones of a book or the soul of a statesman in a few vivid lines'.

Opposite Alfred Harmsworth (1865–1922), a national figure in his twenties and world-famous before he was 40, 'sold news like soap and distributed mad views like stardust'. He amassed titles as well as dividends for four of his seven brothers, who between them collected a viscountcy, a barony and two baronetcies. Harmsworth himself craved nothing so much as to be taken seriously.

rebellious'. They were not written 'by gentlemen for gentlemen': and they most certainly were not written 'by shopgirls for shopgirls', as was said of *The Times* in the 1980s by Dr John Casey. They were capable, according to Cardinal Manning, of 'ennobling as well as entertaining'. They also, said G. B. Shaw, talked about democracy, democratically.

Northcliffe, however, is another story. He was no simple newspaperman, not in the Victorian sense at least. Like his megalomaniacal counterpart in America, W. R. Hearst, he was a fantasist. He lived in a childlike dream world, imagining wonderful stories and then going out and creating them in order to astonish the world. When he launched the *Daily Mail* in 1896, 'his name was synonymous with shallow commercial schemes and cheap publicity stunts'. He was 'not even an innovator, simply an imitator of the worst kind of American journalism'. And 'the amazing success of the *Mail*', according to his chief assistant, Kennedy Jones, 'lay more in its brilliant distribution than in its flashy journalism'. In short, 'The Northoleon of Fleet Street produced marvels out of nothing.'[74] Need more be said in words? Perhaps not. On then, with the picture-show!

9 'From Royal Road to Royal Nightmare'

(Lord Deedes, 1989)

Fleet Street, or 'Brain Street' as George Sala insisted on calling it while it was still 'more or less a habitation of the mind' (H. W. Massingham), began its long history as a royal road to St Paul's and ended, according to Lord Deedes, as a royal nightmare for the newspaper industry. He was not, of course, referring solely to *The Sun*, which then probably gave more grief to the Royal Family than most other newspapers, but to the turbulent tabloids generally. Overmanning, frequent strikes and a refusal to accept new technology at any price were the principal factors producing the proprietorial nightmare.

J. S. Elias, of Odhams Press, became Lord Southwood, the first Labour press baron, in 1937. A business genius if no journalist, and arch-canvasser of insurance schemes and free gifts, he lived to see the circulation of the *Daily Herald* soar to above the 2 million mark (then the largest among the dailies).

Top Left The Press Association and Reuters first occupied the last of the great 'news' buildings in Fleet Street, No. 85, shortly before the Second World War. This building, designed by Sir Edwin Lutyens, still houses the headquarters of Britain's two principal news agencies. Over the arch are the Reuter family arms.

Top Right Edward Hulton (in 1957 to be knighted like his father before him) brought a new honesty as well as excitement to illustrated journalism by launching *Picture Post* in the fraught prewar days of 1938. Here he plans with two of his early contributors, Julian Huxley and L. F. Easterbrook.

Above Bombers would soon be over London, but Fleet Street works on through the night in a blaze of light: *Picture Post* features the *Daily Express* in 1939.

Above Nor does *The Times* see any reason to change its traditional practices in the subs' room: a still from the Paul Rotha documentary film *The Fourth Estate*. This was never shown on public release.

Opposite War has come, and it is the turn of *The Times* to suffer: the scene at Printing House Square on the morning of 25 September 1940.

Left All Fleet Street grieved when St Bride's, 'the Printers' Cathedral', was among the 'Blitz' casualties on the night of 30 December 1940. But Wren's tallest spire, 'a madrigal in stone', survived. Its early Roman history was revealed when archaeologists dug deeply in the ruins. Today, a permanent display in the crypt gives historical perspective to the restored church. The display was presented by Sir Max Aitken in memory of his father, Lord Beaverbrook.

Right   Tom Hopkinson (knighted in 1978) took over the editorship of *Picture Post* from Stefan Lorant, and was the inspiration of much social comment, mainly about the need for a welfare state, during his great years (1940–50).

Below   1942 was a desperate moment of crisis for shipping losses in the Battle of the Atlantic. The *Daily Mirror* came near to being closed down by government order when this cartoon by Philip Zec appeared on 3 March with caption supplied by William Connor. To its millions of readers before and after the war, William Connor was 'Cassandra', the fearless voice of the people. Knighted in 1965, his 'As I was saying when I was interrupted', following victory, became a glorious part of Street legend.

''The price of petrol has been increased by one penny.''—Official.

Above This well-groomed editorial conference is clearly a Kemsley Newspapers affair. On the wall is a map for Mercury, the Foreign and Imperial News Service initiated for Kemsley by Ian Fleming in his pre-James Bond days.

Left When the present Queen and Prince Philip were married in 1947, wartime austerity was set aside and the world's press photographers descended hungrily on London. Royal-watching had now to be shared with television.

Above Left   After the war Astor-family ownership of *The Observer* enabled them to replace the great J. L. Garvin, conservative editor from 1908 to 1942, first by Ivor Brown (1942–8) and then by David Astor (1948–76), the only London proprietor-editor ever to evolve and make work a true political independence.

Above Right   Brendan Bracken, still only 44, became undisputed master of the burgeoning world of financial journalism in 1945, when his *Financial News* acquired *The Financial Times* (adopting the title of the latter). He was created a viscount seven years later.

Opposite Top   Sir Albert Richardson's Bracken House, in Cannon Street – pink-hued like the *FT* it housed – was the first postwar structure to achieve listed status. Its famous 'astronomical' clock, with Winston Churchill at its centre, remains *in situ*.

Opposite Bottom   Hopkinson sent James Cameron and Bert Hardy to the Korean War for *Picture Post*; here is Cameron at the front. The message of their combined photojournalism, brilliant technically, was anathema politically to Hulton, and Hopkinson was dismissed.

Opposite Top Idle printers, 1955: a ten-day national newspaper strike was followed by a short national rail strike, which ended the *Manchester Guardian*'s brief moment of glory as the only 'quality' available everywhere in Britain.

Opposite Bottom The genius of Victor Weisz, alias 'Vicky', adorned in turn the *News Chronicle, Daily Mirror* and *Evening Standard*.

Above The combined *Daily Mail/Evening News* machine room in Northcliffe House, 1956, looking like the engine room of a coal-burning liner.

Left Roy Thomson, later ennobled as the 1st Baron Thomson of Fleet, was, like Beaverbrook, a Canadian industrialist with a driving ambition for press ownership. Unlike Beaverbrook, however, he had little interest in journalism *per se*. He is pictured here in May 1962 with the first pioneer issue of what, after a faltering start, became a resounding success, *The Sunday Times Magazine*. Colour had come into its own at last.

Above In the 1960s, when the new technology was being made available in America, traditional production methods continued in Fleet Street in both the editorial and printing departments; here are *Daily Mail* subs in Northcliffe House.

Right War damage to its premises off Fleet Street forced the *Daily Mirror* to build anew. With Sir Owen Williams designing what is seen as his masterpiece, the Mirror Group Building (1961) in Holborn Circus was the result. Medallions in the lobby are a pleasing gesture to four who have made outstanding contributions to the newspaper's history since its foundation by Northcliffe: Harry Guy Bartholomew, a director from 1913 and the driving force between the wars; King; Cudlipp; and 'Cassandra' (Sir William Connor).

Opposite Top Eyeball to eyeball: a taste of the boardroom battle between Hugh (later Baron) Cudlipp and Cecil King. The autocratic King, nephew of Northcliffe, had been a director of the *Daily Mirror* at 28, and rose to become chairman of the International Publishing Corporation (IPC, which included the *Daily Mirror*). But he was ousted after a revolt led by Cudlipp, his dynamic deputy.

Left Until the cataclysm of Wapping in 1986, the world record production of the *News of the World* still flowed from the linotypes in Bouverie Street. The building was erected in the 1930s ('every stick and stone and piece of steel... of British Empire origin and of British manufacture'), at the same time as those of the *Daily Express* and *The Daily Telegraph* in Fleet Street itself.

149

Opposite Top Left Beset by industrial trouble, *The Times* was closed down by its management for 11 months, from December 1978, at a cost of £40m. Back on the streets in November 1979, its optimism for the immediate future proved illusory.

Opposite Top Right Early confrontation of two later protagonists: in 1969 Robert Maxwell was seeking control of the *News of the World*, but this was snatched from him by Rupert Murdoch, in what was called 'the biggest steal since the Great Train Robbery'.

Opposite Harold Evans, as editor of *The Times:* pictured by Linda Kitson for the penultimate cover in1982 of *Journalism Studies Review*.

Above The triumphant Murdoch: savouring a quiet moment before the News International presses at Wapping rolled again.

Left The barbed wire behind which *The Times, The Sunday Times*, the *News of the World* and *The Sun* first emerged from the Wapping 'factory'; the determined distribution trucks passed through the picket lines equally unscathed.

Far Left The 'stately home' of *The Daily Telegraph* and *The Sunday Telegraph*: Peterborough Court at South Quay, on the Isle of Dogs.

Opposite Bottom The *Telegraph* editorial staff with their VDUs. This new technology became politically acceptable after Rupert Murdoch's defeat of the print unions in 1986.

Top Right Late nineteenth century to latter-day twentieth: three executives of *The Daily Telegraph* inspect one of the two 'masthead' panels preserved from the demolition in Fleet Street. This masthead, bearing the slogan 'Was, Is & Will Be', was designed in 1885 by the College of Heralds at the instigation of the future Lord Burnham.

Left Last presses to run in Fleet Street: the *Daily Express* was printed here on 17 November 1989 for the following day's issue.

10   Milestones and Markers

James Mill

James Mill (1773–1836), stern father of John Stuart Mill (1806–75), is best remembered for this early essay on 'Liberty of the Press', published in *The Edinburgh Review* for May–August 1811.[75] His voluminous writing on philosophical liberalism exerted a profound influence on the political reformers of his day, and especially on his son's famous essay, 'On Liberty', published in 1859.

To point out the exact limits of the power of the press to disorder society by the abuse of censure, would require a minute analysis of the nature and constitution of different governments. A few obvious considerations, however, may be presented, which afford no inaccurate standard to judge by. Of those countries which have enjoyed the most of the power of censure by the press; and those which have enjoyed the least: – in which has there appeared the greatest disposition to anarchy, and in which the least? The answer which the experience of history presents to us, will surprise those who have credulously lent their faith to the men who have lately been so active in traducing the application of censure by the press. The only countries in which any tolerable degree of the liberty of the press has ever been enjoyed, have been a few of the Protestant countries of modern times – England, Holland, Switzerland, and the United States of North America. Now, so far from showing the greatest tendency to anarchy, – of all countries that ever existed, these have been the farthest removed from that tendency. In what country in Europe is there so much tendency to insurrection, as in Turkey? And what other countries of Europe have the most nearly resembled Turkey in that particular? We answer – Italy; and whatever country has shared the most in that despotism which Italy exercised upon the thoughts and expressions of the people.

But the revolution of France is something which agitates the imaginations of men, and which, without allowing them time to render themselves in any tolerable degree acquainted with the facts of that extraordinary event, makes them fear and detest in the mass all things which, justly or unjustly, have been ever supposed to have had a share in producing it. The abuse of the press was carried to a great height during the excesses of the French revolution; – the abuse, therefore, of the press was, they tell us, the cause of these excesses. This we consider to be the fallacy, or mistake of the judgment, which, in classing and demonstrating the sophisms, Aristotle called το πη αίτιον ώs αίτιον—*non causa pro causa*. The abuses of the press which attended the excesses of the French revolution, we regard as the effect not the cause of the public disorders. It will not be asserted, that public discontent and public insurrection were not more frequent before there was a press than since. Now, suppose that, by the progress of such discontent, the bands of government had become nearly as dissolved as they were in France at the time of the assembling of the

States General; will any considerate man take upon him to say that the same, or as great, excesses might not have taken place had no press existed? Were there never any cruel and sanguinary revolutions, but where there was a press? It would really appear as if the terror of the French revolution had paralyzed the understandings as well as extinguished the public virtues of a great number of men.

Mr Burke, who, though his lights were not very steady, saw by glances a great way into the structure and play of the machines of society, has well described those turbulent spirits who, by means of the press, or by any other means, are in danger of becoming the authors of mischief in a revolution. 'A species of men,' says he, 'to whom a state of order would become a sentence of obscurity, are nourished into a dangerous magnitude by the heat of intestine disturbances; and it is no wonder that, by a sort of sinister piety, they cherish, in their turn, the disorders which are the parents of all their consequence.' To the prevalence, in France, of such men as these, and to the abuse of the press, has the revolution and all its evil consequences been ascribed. Now, what says Mr Burke on this important question? 'Superficial observers,' says he, 'consider such persons as the *cause* of the public uneasiness, when, in truth, they are nothing more than the *effect*.' This is a truth of prodigious importance; of which Burke himself but too easily and too completely, at an after period, lost sight; and by his eloquence, induced too many others to follow his example. The expressions which immediately followed in the same passage are not less remarkable, nor less at variance with subsequent doctrines of the same writer. 'Good men,' says he, 'look upon this distracted scene with sorrow and indignation. They stand in a most distressing alternative. But, in the election among evils, they hope better things from *temporary confusion*, than from *established servitude*.'

There is another grievous mistake involved in this prejudice with regard to the matter of fact. It was not the abuse of a *free* press which was witnessed during the French revolution; it was the abuse of an *enslaved* press. The press was at all times the exclusive instrument of the domineering faction, who made use of it to calumniate their enemies and agitate the people; but prevented, by the terrors of extermination, all other men from making use of the press to expose their machinations and character. It was exactly that species of abuse which is committed, in different degrees, by every set of rulers in France, in England, or any where else, who allow more latitude to freedom of expression on their own side, than on that of their opponents. Had real freedom of the press been enjoyed – had the honest men whom France contained been left a channel by which to lay their sentiments before the public – had a means been secured of instructing the people in the real nature of the delusions which were practised upon them, the enormities of the revolution would have been confined within a narrow compass, and its termination would have been very different. . . .

If men would only employ a little patient consideration in forming their notions, we should not despair of getting all but a few, to join with us in opinion, that, so far from the freedom of the press being the cause of the French revolution, had a free press existed in France, the French revolution never would have taken place. It is the natural, nay, we may confidently say, the necessary effect of a free press, so to harmonize together the tone of the government and the

sentiments of the people, that no jarring opposition between them can ever arise. By the free circulation of opinions, the government is always fully appraised, which, by no other means, it ever can be, of the sentiments of the people, and feels a decided interest in conforming to them. As it must thus, in some degree, mould itself upon the sentiments of the people, so it feels an interest in fashioning the sentiments of the people to a conformity with its views. It is at pains to instruct, to persuade, and to conciliate. It acts not with a proud and negligent disdain of the feelings of the people. In a word, the government and the people are under a moral necessity of acting together; a free press compels them to bend to one another; and any contrariety of views and purposes liable to arise, can never come to such a head as to threaten convulsions. We may safely affirm, that more freedom of the press granted to our own country, would have the salutary effect of harmonizing, to a much greater degree, the tone of government and the sentiments of the people, and of rendering all violent opposition between them still more improbable than even at present it is. We may even go further: we may speak of that state of convulsion itself, against which so many of our contemporaries think it necessary to take so many precautions. Were that revolution, which we think so very little probable, really to happen, nothing would prove so strong a bulwark against the abuses, to which a state of revolution is apt to give birth, as the freedom of the press, so clearly established and modified by law, and the utility of its exercise so fully proved by experience, that it would be impossible for the public to be deceived in regard to the shackles which a predominant faction might desire to impose upon that freedom, or in regard to the false glosses which it would endeavour to put upon its and other men's transactions.

That the press, too, though calculated to produce important effects in the slow progress of ages, is an instrument with which no violent and sudden changes can ever be effected, we should think abundantly evident, upon a little consideration of its very nature. This is a circumstance which did not escape the sagacity of Mr Hume, and which, though cautious and timid with respect to government, even to a degree, as Mr Fox justly remarks, of womanish imbecility, he hesitated not to express in several of the first editions of his Essays. The point is so well handled by him, and his authority is so high, that we prefer delivering our sentiments upon it, in his words, to our own. 'Since, therefore,' says Mr Hume, 'the liberty of the press is so essential to the support of our mixed government, this sufficiently decides the question, whether this liberty be advantageous or prejudicial; there being nothing of greater importance in every state than the preservation of the antient government, especially if it be a free one. But I would fain go a step further, and assert, that such a liberty is attended with so few inconveniences, that it may be claimed as the common right of mankind, and ought to be indulged them almost in every government; except the ecclesiastical, to which indeed it would be fatal. We need not dread, from this liberty, any such ill consequences as followed from the harangues of the popular demagogues of Athens, and tribunes of Rome. A man reads a book or pamphlet alone and coolly. There is none present from whom he can catch the passion by contagion. He is not hurried away by the force and energy of action. And, should he be wrought up to never so seditious a humour, there is no violent resolution presented to him, by which he can immediately vent his passion. The liberty of the press, therefore, however abused, can scarce ever excite popular tumults or rebellion. And as

to those murmurs or secret discontents it may occasion, 'tis better they should get vent in words, that they may come to the knowledge of the magistrate before it be too late, in order to his providing a remedy against them. Mankind, 'tis true, have always a greater propension to believe what is said to the disadvantage of their governors, than the contrary; but this inclination is inseparable from them, whether they have liberty or not. A whisper may fly as quick, and be as pernicious, as a pamphlet. Nay, it will be more pernicious, where men are not accustomed to think freely, or distinguish betwixt truth and falsehood.'

Here, for the present, we must suspend our observations. On some of the most important topics connected with the subject, we have been altogether unable to touch. We have not been able to mention any of the considerations which prescribe, as well as fix, the limits within which the liberty of the press should be confined. But we promise not to lose sight of the subject. The liberty of the press is a point on which so much depends, and with regard to which there is still in this country so much room for reform, that we shall not be easily induced to remit our efforts, till that sort of legislative provision, which we have here endeavoured to describe, be at last bestowed upon the nation.

P. L. Simmonds

P. L. Simmonds (1814–97) was an orphan, born in Lund, Sweden, and adopted by a British naval officer, George Simmonds, with whom he lived in the West Indies until 1834. His name appears for the first time in England as editor of the *East Hampshire Repository* in 1836. There was also a *Simmonds Colonial Magazine* (1840–53). But his most useful contribution to press history was his compilation of newspaper statistics for that most 'opaque' period, 1782–1840. It was read before the Statistical Society of London on 21 June 1841. It begins:

It is worthy of observation, that the History and Statistics of the Newspaper Press, and of Periodical Literature in general, have occupied a very small share of public attention. This will appear the more remarkable, when we consider the popularity of the subject, its interesting features, and the important bearings and influence of this portion of the Press upon society. It may be that the vast extent of the newspaper press, the facility with which these ephemeral sheets may be consulted, and the regular manner in which intelligence from all lands is brought home by their aid to our own firesides, with a degree of correctness and speed unparalleled in the history of bygone ages, make them to be comparatively slighted, after the manner of the adage – that familiarity breeds contempt. Were they more scarce and inaccessible, their importance would perhaps be better estimated, and their influence and benefits more highly appreciated.

It is a strange anomaly, that in England alone, newspaper writers are looked down upon as an

inferior caste of literati; and that the purveyors of intelligence, whose especial business is to inform and instruct the public – who must of necessity be men of diversified talent, and extensive knowledge – who are in many cases individuals of superior literary attainments – and who are generally the first to publish and make known important inventions and scientific improvements – whose judgment, moreover, is to approve or condemn works, treating often of the most exalted or most abstruse subjects, – are themselves a proscribed race. And yet, at no former period perhaps, was the Newspaper Press so popular, or in such high repute and importance as at the present time. This is more especially the case in France and in England. In the former country, the pens of the greatest men and most talented authors are continually engaged on periodical literature. There is, however, this marked difference between the two countries, that in France the writers, with an honest pride, generally append their names to the articles which they contribute. M. M. Thiers, Guizot, B. Constant, Chateaubriand, Arago, and De Villèle have been frequent contributors to newspapers; – while in England, to identify a distinguished public man, or an eminent author as a newspaper writer, would be considered a decided insult. And yet the secret history of the English newspapers, if laid bare, would display a host of talent, and an array of distinguished names, that would scarcely be credited by those who are not acquainted with the subject.

If newspapers be, as we believe they are, one of the best criterions of the intelligence and commercial prosperity of a nation, it follows that an enquiry into the subject must be attended with beneficial results, particularly in a statistical point of view. The Newspaper Press presents a wide and interesting field of observation; and an examination into the channels of intelligence and information possessed by different countries, treating of their number, literary and political character, freedom of discussions, whether fettered, or not, by fiscal and legal restrictions, typography, price, antiquity, &c., would form a curious index to the civilization, commercial prosperity, and literary taste and talent of the various nations of the world. Even as a bare index for reference to authors, advertisers, and politicians – setting aside its statistical importance – it would not be without its advantages. The history, too, of Newspapers is intimately interwoven with the historical annals of every country, exemplifying the progress of literature and science, and throwing much light upon the state of society and the philosophy of the times in which they were published. It is therefore surprising that the Newspaper Press has not yet found its historian. A few casual papers, in magazines, concerning portions only of the subject, and written rather with a view to amuse than to instruct, are all that have ever yet appeared. The subject, as a whole, remains untouched, and is untrodden ground for any adventurous mind to examine and explore. It is indeed a vast field, which, from the importance of its various relations, can scarcely be grasped by any single individual, without the co-operation of other parties, and the contemporaneous assistance of those literary societies which every principal continental town now possesses.

In England, at the time of the reduction of the stamp on newspapers to one penny, the subject of the press was necessarily thrust prominently before the public eye; but the attention it arrested was momentary and fleeting, and after the object for which it had been agitated was

attained, and a few ably-written articles had appeared, entering somewhat more minutely than heretofore into the statistics of the London and provincial press, the matter dropped once more into comparative oblivion. The only existing index to the press of Great Britain is the meagre broad sheet published occasionally by some of the London newspaper agents, which is generally very imperfect. As to the press of other countries, little or nothing is known. Some occasional traveller, when he publishes his observations on men and manners, may now and then incidentally allude to the newspapers of the countries which he visits, but few take any trouble to obtain information on this head that may be depended upon, or consulted with advantage.

In the belief that even a cursory glance at the newspaper press of the world will, in the absence of more extensive information, be acceptable to the members of the Statistical Society of London, we shall proceed to lay before them an outline of the subject, to the extent which our information will permit.

France, America, England, and Germany are the countries in which newspapers flourish in the greatest number. Our present limits will not permit us to enter into any minute particulars; but we shall pass in review the press of different countries, and state, where attainable, the progress that has been made by each in this branch of literature during the last half-century.

As in most other questions of importance, the claimants for the honour of the first printed newspaper have been numerous; France, Germany, Italy, and England have severally contested the priority. Until within a very late period, England had established, on what was believed to be conclusive and satisfactory evidence, her title to the disputed honour. 'The *English Mercurie*, published by authoritie for the prevention of false reports,' 'imprinted at London by her Highness' printer, in 1588,' of which three or four numbers are preserved in the British Museum, was supposed to be a genuine publication.

The claim, however, has recently, upon evidence which cannot be gainsaid, been found to be untenable, and the merit of priority in the publication of printed newspapers, like the authorship of the Letters of Junius, will probably ever remain undecided, a fruitful field for debate and disputation.

The United Kingdom. – London, as the capital, and most populous city of the British Isles, has always been the centre from which the largest number and the most influential papers have emanated. When we look back to the sources of information possessed by our forefathers, scarcely two centuries ago, we are astonished at the inferiority of the channels of intelligence of those days. In 1696, we are informed that there were but 9 newspapers published in London, all of them appearing at weekly intervals. In 1709 the number of papers in London had increased to 18, of which only one was published daily. In 1724 the number was 3 daily, 6 weekly, 7 three times a week, '3 half-penny Posts,' and the *London Gazette*, twice a week.

The following Table will shew their subsequent progression:

YEARS	Number of Newspapers Published in				
	London	*England and Wales and British Islands*	Scotland	Ireland	Total
1782	18	50	8	3	79
1792	42	70	14	—	—
1795	38	72	13	35	158
1809	63	93	24	37	217
1815	55	122	26	49	252
1830	54	154	36	60	304
1833	55	183	46	75	369
1836	55	183	46	75	369
1837	85	237	65	71	458
1838	88	224	56	77	445
1839	124†	237	66	89	516
1840	109†	224	70	90	493

†These are computed from the Stamp Returns for the last quarter of the year, and include several literary journals and price currents, which are not strictly newspapers; about 90 or 100 may be fairly considered newspapers.

In 1792 there were in London 13 daily and 20 semi-weekly and weekly papers. In 1795 there were 14 daily, 10 three times a week, 2 twice a week, and 12 weekly. The amount of revenue which they yielded to government in 1788 was 129,000*l.* In 1790 the number of copies of papers printed was 14,035,639. From August 1791 to August 1792, the number printed was 14,794,193, which yielded to government 118,498*l.* The number in the following year, ended August 1793, was 17,073,621, which produced 142,280*l.* In 1824 the number of copies of newspapers published weekly, was about 500,000, or 26,000,000 in the year.

In 1836 (year ended 15th September), when the Stamp duty was 4*d.*, the total number of stamps issued for the United Kingdom was 35,576,056. In 1839 (ending at the same period), the total number of 1*d.* stamps issued, was as follows:–

London	29,127,583
English provincial papers	19,905,801
England and Wales	49,033,384
Scotland	3,974,444
Ireland	5,509,034
Total	58,516,862

The consumption of stamps has therefore increased 64 per cent., or nearly two-thirds, since the reduction of the duty. In London there are about 100 different newspapers published, but the number varies continually, as many start into existence and are continued only for a few weeks:

some have been established for nearly a century; others from 50 to 60 years. The oldest existing London papers are the *English Chronicle, or White-hall Evening Post*, which was commenced in 1747; the *St. James's Chronicle*, 1761; the *Morning Chronicle*, 1769.

The oldest existing English provincial papers are the *Lincoln Mercury*, published at Stamford, 1695; *York Courant*, 1700; *Kentish Gazette*, 1703; *Worcester Journal*, 1709; *Newcastle Courant*, 1711; *Northampton Mercury*, 1720; *Gloucester Journal*, 1720; *Reading Mercury*, 1722; *Chester Courant*, 1733; *Ipswich Journal*, 1737; *Birmingham Gazette*, 1741; *Bath Journal*, 1742; *Derby Mercury*, 1742; all of which have a large circulation, and are highly respectable journals. Besides these there are not more than a dozen that date back earlier than the commencement of the present century.

The oldest paper in Ireland appears to be the *Belfast News-Letter*, which was commenced the 1st of September, 1737. Next to this in antiquity rank the *Limerick Chronicle*, 1744; the Dublin papers, the *News-Letter*, and *Freeman's Journal*, 1765; *Waterford Chronicle*, 1766; *Dublin Evening Post*, 1774. All the other papers are of modern origin.

In Scotland, the *Caledonian Mercury*, Edinburgh, professes to be the oldest existing paper, dating from 1660, but this is not quite correct. The paper at present published under that name is not the original *Mercurius Caledonius*, and was only commenced in 1720, so that it has many seniors – for instance, the *Edinburgh Evening Courant*, 1705. Out of Edinburgh, the oldest papers are the *Aberdeen Journal*, January 1748; *Glasgow Courier*, 1 September 1791; and *Kelso Mail*, 1796.

Henry Reeve and W. R. Greg

Henry Reeve (1813–95) had just started his long period as editor of *The Edinburgh Review* when a row broke out between him and his former employers, *The Times*, over this grandiloquent book review covering the mid-Victorian 'Newspaper Press', published in October 1855. It was thought to be 'needlessly offensive' and it was assumed (wrongly) that Reeve had written it out of spite. In fact, it was written by William Rathbone Greg (1809–81), Manchester-born businessman and prize-winning essayist. The evidence for this, according to the *Wellesley Index*, is in Longman's account book which gives the title of the article, the contributor, his rate of pay, date of payment and, in addition, provides an index by

author to the articles. It was Greg's special function, says Reeve in his memoirs, 'to discourage unreasonable expectations from political or even social reforms cautioning democracy against the abuse of its power'. Certainly, there was no class feeling about Greg, even when he may seem to be advocating the cause of a class.

In common with everything of signal strength, Journalism is a plant of slow and gradual growth. The Fourth Estate, like the Third Estate, has reached its present dimensions and its actual power from slight beginnings, by continuous accretions, and through a long course of systematic and unremitting encroachments. Of far more modern date than the other estates of the realm, it has overshadowed and surpassed them all. It has created the want which it supplies. It has obtained paramount influence and authority partly by assuming them, but still more by deserving them. Of all *puissances* in the political world, it is at once the mightiest, the most irresponsible, the best administered, and the least misused. And, taken in its history, position, and relations, it is unquestionably the most grave, noticeable, formidable phenomenon – the 'greatest FACT' – of our times.

The earliest periodical newspaper published in this country was, 'The Weekly Newes,' which appeared in 1622, under the auspices of one Nathaniel Buttler. It seems to have been almost exclusively devoted to such intelligence as the editor could collect, and to have meddled little with polemics. Indeed, at that time, and down to a much later period, the political warfare of the Press was carried on chiefly by means of pamphlets, of which not less than thirty thousand were issued between 1640 and 1660. During the contests between Charles I and his Parliament, however, Peter Heylin established a weekly journal to advocate the Royal cause; and Matthew Needham, whom Disraeli calls 'the great patriarch of newspaper writers,' followed the example, and started the 'Mercurius Britannicus,' in the Parliamentary interest; then the 'Mercurius Politicus,' on behalf of the popular party, when this had finally become lord of the ascendant. In 1663 Roger L'Estrange set on foot the 'Public Intelligencer,' which was soon merged in or superseded by the 'London Gazette,' – a publication entirely under Government control, and giving or withholding the most important occurrences according to the fancies or interests of the Court. In 1679, however, L'Estrange again appeared as a journalist, having established the 'Observator,' – a paper chiefly distinguished for its virulent and malignant Toryism, and lasting about seven years. Mr. Blakey states – we know not on what authority – that, at one period of the reign of Charles II, the number of newspapers had increased to seventy; few of which, however, had more than an ephemeral existence.

With the fall of the censorship in the reign of William, newspapers naturally grew more numerous, more able, and more powerful; but it was not till the subsequent reign that Journalism assumed the peculiar form and character which it has generally since retained. 'The publication of regular newspapers, partly designed for the communication of intelligence, partly for the discussion of political topics, may be referred, on the whole, to the reign of Anne, when

they obtained great circulation and became the accredited organs of different factions.' At the same period, also, grew up the habit of reporting with more or less regularity and fulness the debates in Parliament. Nearly at the same time, too, was imposed that Stamp Duty which, after several modifications, we have just seen repealed. But the most remarkable feature connected with the Periodical Press at the commencement of the last century, is to be found in the eminence, both for character, position, and ability, of those who shared in its conduct. Journals and pamphlets began to be looked to by men in power as more efficient means of public influence than even eloquence or office; and Members of Parliament, Ministers of State, and literary magnates did not disdain themselves to become journalists and pamphleteers. The 'Examiner,' the 'Whig Examiner,' the 'Medley,' the 'Crisis,' the 'Englishman,' the 'Craftsman,' – to say nothing of periodicals only partially, or not at all, political, – such as the 'Spectator,' 'Guardian,' 'Tatler,' &c. – appeared in rapid succession, devoted to the furtherance of special party views, and conducted by the ablest writers of the day; among whom we need only name Atterbury, Swift, Prior, Addison, Steele, Pulteney, and Bolingbroke.

From this period till the advent of Junius, newspaper literature suffered a strange degeneracy and eclipse: though both Fielding and Smollett were employed, nothing worth noting or remembering seems to have been produced; and even the attention temporarily aroused by the 'North Briton' of Wilkes was due solely to its scurrility, and to the folly of the Government of the day, who contrived, by their ill-judged and relentless persecutions, to make a martyr out of the lowest and dirtiest materials ever used for such a purpose. It was in 1769 that Junius commenced that celebrated series of papers in the 'Public Advertiser,' which not only at the time created a startling excitement, such as no periodical writing, before or since, has ever caused, but produced consequences which are felt even to our day. The 'Letters of Junius' complete that collection of causes and influences to which the journalism of Great Britain, in this second half of the nineteenth century, owes its character and position. He set the example of that union of accurate and secret political information, consummate ability, daring liberty, and pungent and racy style, which has ever since distinguished the highest organs of the newspaper press. Nothing can be said in defence of his inveterate rancour, ferocious partisanship, and unscrupulous personality, – except, indeed, such apology as may be found in the shameless corruption of the time; but in spite of these flagrant faults, he was the uncompromising champion of national morality and freedom, at a period when both were menaced; and though we must regret that his weapon should have been poisoned as well as polished, and barbed as well as keen, it cannot be denied that it was generally directed against adversaries who deserved no quarter. And no one who compares the servile timidity of public writers before Junius took up his pen with the courage and determination which, since his time, they have never lost, will be disposed to make light of the permanent service which his resolute and independent spirit rendered to his country and his craft. 'At the commencement of his career this same writer, before he had assumed the name under which he has become immortal, had furnished Woodfall with a report of one of Burke's speeches in the House of Commons. The report was covered with the usual disguise of a speech at

a debating society: and, as it is the earliest, so it is the tamest, of Burke's reported speeches. Yet Woodfall dared not publish it without several omissions and alterations. Two years later the same printer published, without hesitation, Junius's "Letter to the King." '

The progress of the Newspaper Press, in extent, influence, and reputation, from that period to the present, has been marked and steady; but we need not follow its details. A sort of chronic war was kept up between the Government and the Journals during the whole reign of George III; and this and the alteration of the Law of Libel by the famous Bill of Mr. Fox, completed the emancipation of the Periodical Press from all fetters but such as decency and patriotism combine to sanction and maintain.

'This chapter (writes Mr. Hunt) is headed with the title of "a newspaper of 1688 and one of 1788." The "Orange Intelligencer" started in the year of the Revolution. The first number of the "Times" appeared exactly a hundred years afterwards, and they may therefore stand as two boundary marks, indicating the extremes of a century of newspaper history. Let us see what that century had done for such publications. The "Intelligencer," though set up at a time of great political importance, was small in size and consisted of two pages, about the size of the "Penny Magazine." The No. of Dec. 11. 1688 boasts of two advertisements; a small paragraph amongst its news describes the seizing of Jefferies in his attempt to escape from the anger of his enemies; it has sixteen lines of intelligence from Ireland, and eight from Scotland, whilst under its news of England we have not very much more. One of the items tells us that "On the 7th instant the Prince of Orange supt at the Bear Inn, Hungerford.... The first No. of the "Times" is dated January, 1788, and its price is marked threepence. Compared with the first No. of the "Intelligencer" of 1688, No. 1. of the new journal is a giant. It contains ten times as much matter; it has four pages, each of four columns, somewhat smaller than the "Globe" and "Standard" now present; it has sixty-three advertisements, foreign as well as home intelligence, poetry, shipping news, and paragraphs of gossip, some of them rather doubtful in character.'

Three quarters of a century have elapsed, and the 'Times' of 1855 has outstripped the 'Times' of 1788 as much as this had done its predecessor of 1688. It contains *ninety-six* columns of the size we are all familiar with; the fullest and amplest information from every quarter of the world; admirable writing on every subject of the day on which any interest is felt; frequent literary criticisms of masterly talent and unimpeachable independence; full reports of all debates and transactions in Parliament; and, to crown the whole, not fewer on an average than *two thousand* advertisements daily. In 1753 (we quote from Mr. Hunt) the aggregate newspaper circulation was 7,411,757; in 1792 it had reached 15,005,760; in 1836, before the reduction in the stamp duty, the issue in Great Britain was above 29,000,000; in 1837, after that reduction, 42,000,000; in 1848, 67,000,000 for England, and 7,500,000 for Scotland. In the year 1849, the total number of Journals in the United Kingdom was 547. The number, in 1851, had still further increased, and the stamps issued had risen to 91,600,000....

Probably the most important of the victories gained for the 'freedom of unlicensed printing' was the enactment of Mr. Fox's law of libel in 1792, leaving to the jury the right of deciding on the character of the thing published as well as on the fact of publication. The value of this measure

was amply proved during the stormy period of the next twenty years; but many reminiscences will serve to show that the perfect liberty of utterance we now enjoy was not won till long afterwards, and by slow degrees. It is curious to us in these times to recall that in 1799 the 'Courier' was prosecuted, and its conductors fined and imprisoned, for saying that 'the Emperor of Russia was a tyrant among his subjects, and ridiculous to the rest of Europe.' In 1803, on the charge of Perceval, and in spite of the defence of Mackintosh, Peltier was found guilty of a libel on Bonaparte, and only escaped sentence by the renewal of the war. In 1810, the 'Chronicle' and the 'Examiner' were prosecuted for saying that 'of all monarchs since the Revolution, the successor of George III. will have the finest opportunity of becoming popular.' The Jury, however, refused to convict. In the following year the 'Examiner' was again prosecuted for an article against flogging in the army, but with a similar result. Another prosecution for personal ridicule of the Prince Regent was more successful, for Leigh Hunt and his brother, the editors, were fined and imprisoned. From returns laid before Parliament, it appears that between 1808 and 1821 the number of persons prosecuted for political libels written or spoken, on *ex officio* informations, was 101; and the aggregate amount of imprisonment inflicted was 171 years! And, finally, a return, dated 1830, 'of all prosecutions during the reign of George III. and George IV., either by *ex officio* information or indictment, under the direction of the attorney or solicitor-general, for libels or other misdemeanours against members of the Government or other persons acting in an official capacity,' gives a sum total of twenty-five. Fifty years ago the most moderate severity of criticism, and the most legitimate latitude of discussion, sufficed to draw down the vindictive notice of the Government: now, it is difficult to conceive that any extravagance of vituperation, short of actual slander as to matters of fact, would provoke the most touchy or foolish minister to file an information or lay an indictment against a public journal.

Thus by gradual steps, and through much tribulation, the newspaper press of England has attained to the mighty influence which it now exercises. That influence it is scarcely possible to exaggerate. Journalism is now truly an estate of the realm; more powerful than any of the other estates; more powerful than all of them combined if it could ever be brought to act as a united and concentrated whole. Nor need we wonder at its sway. It furnishes the daily reading of millions. It furnishes the exclusive reading of hundreds of thousands. Not only does it supply the nation with nearly all the information on public topics which it possesses, but it supplies it with its notions and opinions in addition. It furnishes not only the materials on which our conclusions must be founded: it furnishes the conclusions themselves, cut and dried – coined, stamped, and polished. It inquires, reflects, decides for us. For five pence or a penny (as the case may be) it *does all the thinking* of the nation; saves us the trouble of weighing and perpending, of comparing and deliberating; and presents us with ready-made opinions clearly and forcibly expressed. For the number of those who form their own conclusions on public matters independently of their newspapers, or who take the trouble or risk perplexity of reading more newspapers than one, are few indeed, and are chiefly to be found in the metropolis.

The power of journalism, vast and preponderating as it is, is not greater than it deserves. If at times we grow alarmed at its extent, we cannot, on calm reflection, deny that it has been well

earned and richly merited. The newspaper press owes its influence to three causes, – to the special value of the functions which it exercises; to the remarkable talent with which it is habitually conducted; and to the generally high and pure character which it maintains.

In the first place, it is a necessary portion, complement, and guardian of free institutions. In a country where the people – *i.e.* the great mass of the educated classes – govern, where they take that ceaseless and paramount interest in public affairs which is at once the inseparable symptom and the surest safeguard of political and civil liberty, where, in a word, they are participating citizens, not passive subjects, of the State, – it is of the most essential consequence that they should be furnished from day to day with the materials requisite for informing their minds and enlightening their judgment. If they are in any degree to control, to guide, to stimulate the administration, they must, as far as possible, become qualified to do so. They need, therefore, to be kept *au courant* of all transactions and events which bear upon the interests or credit of their country.

But as bare facts without careful analysis or suggestive commentary would be profitless and undigestible to all save the trained and cultivated few, and as most of us are too busy in the daily avocations of our own career to have leisure, even if we had talent, for patient pondering and meditation, it is essential that the reading and reigning people should be furnished, in addition to the raw material of narrative, with such clear criticisms and such condensed dissertations as the keenest and best qualified intellects of the country can supply. To make up our minds promptly and decidedly on matters of public policy or on the conduct of public men is no easy task for any but those trained to the work. The mass, even of the comparatively cultivated and enlightened, will always need extraneous aid in the performance of this task; and journalists here discharge somewhat the same functions as the pleadings of the advocate and the summary of the judge in our courts of law. They arrange, collate, condense, and expound for the benefit of the listening jury, calling attention to what might have been overlooked, pointing out what is important and what irrelevant, clearing up what is obscure, explaining what is technical, and placing before the audience the matter for consideration in a prepared form and in the clearest and most instructive light.

Again: Journalism is needed as part and parcel of the *representation* of the country. The House of Commons is not, and perhaps never can be made, a complete and perfect representative of all classes, all interests, all shades of opinion. Certainly it has not yet realised that bright ideal. Non-electors are more numerous than electors. Thousands of Englishmen of nearly every rank – dwellers in towns that are not boroughs, dwellers in counties who are not freeholders nor large tenants, residents in cities who are not householders – have no members of Parliament to listen to them and to speak for them. The holders of unusual opinions, or of moderate or philosophic doctrines, the votaries of 'coming' creeds, the members of minorities in a word, are unrepresented in Parliament, unless by some happy accident. The House of Commons, too, is even more inadequate and insufficient than it is incomplete and partial as a representation of the acting, thinking, stirring, discussing crowds of political Englishmen. It sits only half the year. It is overwhelmed with details of business. It cannot suffice to give utterance to half the thoughts

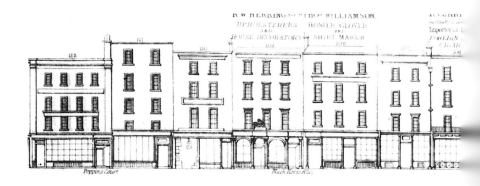

that are bursting for expression, or to ask half the questions that the country is burning to have answered. Moreover, chosen as it is; fettered as it is by peculiar rules; managed as it is by skilful politicians, experienced in all its potent and suppressing forms; composed as it is necessarily of men who, however they may habitually share the popular sentiments, have by virtue of the seat, as a mere consequence of being there, interests and wishes not always in harmony with those of their constituents (as, for example, when any questions are in agitation which might involve a dissolution), – the House of Commons is often ostensibly, and far oftener in reality, at variance with the prevalent feeling of the nation, or of some powerful section of it. We all feel that we could not do without the vent for expression which the Newspaper Press affords us. We should explode were it not for such an immediate and ample safety-valve. We could not possibly wait for the slow expression, the inadequate and inaccurate exposition of our sentiments and opinions which only could be furnished to us by our senators in St. Stephens! It is not too much to say that if by any accident journalism were to become suddenly extinct, such a Parliamentary Reform as the wildest of us have never dreamed of, would become an instant and paramount necessity. Those who have no share in the choice of members, those who feel themselves inadequately represented or misrepresented, those who find in Parliament none who hold their peculiar doctrines or who are qualified to give them effective utterance, – would all join to insist upon such an entire renovation and reconstitution of the representative assembly as would throw all previous 'organic changes' into the shade.

But perhaps one of the most necessary and practically important functions of the Daily Press is the opening it affords for the exposition of individual grievances and wrongs. It is a surer guarantee against injustice and oppression than any institutions or any forms of government could be. Even the freest and most popular executive wields fearful instruments of quiet and insensible tyranny which the victims of them could neither escape nor resist, but which they may expose. Courts of justice are tedious and costly; thousands can neither 'wait the law's delay nor resist the oppressor's wrong;' instances, too, of harshness and iniquity every day occur of which the law can take no cognisance, and which would have no chance of hearing or redress, were it not for that tribunal which is always open, which is open gratuitously, which is open to every complainant. Neglected or unrewarded merit, which can obtain no audience from men in power; long services which have been discarded or superseded to make way for the high-born or the favoured; sufferers under unjust and brutal exertions of undeniable power and right, – all these can make their appeal to a judge whose authority is the greatest, and to a court whose publicity is the widest in the realm. In Great Britain scarcely any public or private iniquity can be done 'in a corner;' silence can never be counted upon; secrecy even is never safe. Every man of any note acts under a vigilant and daring eye; every public appointment, which 'members' might be influenced to pass by, is certain to be canvassed by a press which refuses to be shackled by the etiquettes and courtesies of social intercourse; every ministerial act, which 'the House,' itself often a sinner, would perhaps condone, is exposed to criticism and interrogatories which corruption cannot face with courage or impunity. In the newspaper, every individual Englishman possesses a protector whose value cannot be exaggerated, and that aggregate of individuals

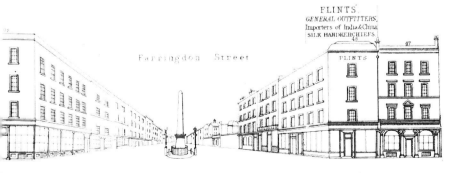

FLINTS
GENERAL OUTFITTERS,
Importers of India & China
SILK HANDKERCHIEFS

which we call the public possesses a guardian of its interests which no power can silence, no money can corrupt, and no flattery can lull to sleep.

The services rendered by the 'fourth estate' to the Government are scarcely less necessary or important than those which it renders to the People. It supplies the latter with a safe channel for the expression of those feelings which might else find a vent in overt acts of discontent and insubordination, and it keeps the former cognisant of popular sentiments and passions which it is most essential it should understand and be early made acquainted with. It would be very difficult for even the best intentioned administration to be thoroughly well informed as to the state of feeling and opinion in the nation, except through the medium of the various and discrepant organs of the daily and weekly press. The House of Commons can only most imperfectly supply this information; often its members themselves learn the wishes of their constituents principally or exclusively through this unrecognised channel. In fact, newspapers are just as truly representatives of the people as legal senators, only they attain their rank by a different mode of choice: in the latter case, they are elected beforehand by the people; in the former they nominate themselves, but can retain their seat and exercise their functions only if their nomination be confirmed. If a member of the fourth estate differs with his constituents and incurs their displeasure, he must abdicate or recant as surely as a member of the Lower House, and far more promptly. He is not even allowed to wait till a dissolution.

The value of Journalism as a safety-valve in moderating discontent by allowing it a vent, in expending the energies and exposing the weaknesses and fallacies of demagogues, and in thus preserving the peace and order of society through the joint securities of freedom and of justice, can only be fully estimated by governments which have tried the opposite scheme, or observers who have closely watched its operation. The doubt, the fear, the conscious ignorance, the consequent errors and exaggerated fancies of the governments of countries where the Press is gagged, constitute at once the inevitable consequence and the appropriate punishment of that foolish sin. There is panic because there is darkness; there is tyranny because there is terror. Here, thanks to our many-headed and unfettered Press, the authorities are amply informed, and they are informed in time. They have early warning when they are treading in paths in which public sympathy will not go with them, and tending towards proceedings for which the popular voice would not grant them absolution. In a country which has reached that stage of freedom and self-government on which England now stands, ministers must govern in conformity with the will of the effective body of the nation; and how can they ascertain this save through those great organs of utterance which sometimes form and sometimes express the general opinion, but can never be ignorant of it or out of harmony with it?

But the Periodical Press is invaluable to the Government in another way. Through it ministers can instruct and inoculate the nation. They, as well as their critics and antagonists, have access to its columns. It is an engine which they or their friends can use as effectually as it can be used against them. By its means they may prepare the public mind for a great measure, educate it to the understanding of a complicated subject, penetrate it to the core with some healing or prolific principle, clear up misconceptions, defend themselves against slanderous accusations, insin-

uate needful elucidations and explanations which yet could not well have been officially supplied. In those few cases in which the Government has been in advance of the people (the new Poor Law was one), by using the Press as an instrument of education, it has made that possible which might otherwise have been attempted in vain.

Finally, newspapers are of the utmost service to Government in completing and correcting its official information. They have now reached a pitch of wealth and talent which enables them to command wider, abler, and more numerous channels in every quarter of the world than are often open to the agents of Government. It may seem strange and scarely creditable that it should be so, but the fact is undeniable that the leading journals for many years past have communicated tidings of important events to the public before those tidings had reached ministers through their ordinary official correspondence. The more agitating the crisis, and the more momentous the news, the more likely is it to be early received by those whose profession, pride, and interest it is to obtain it and publish it with marvellous rapidity. Not only is newspaper intelligence often earlier and fuller than that transmitted through official channels: it is also frequently more correct. We can scarcely be surprised at this; the sinister interests are on the whole less strong, and the public is a sterner task-master than the administration. The correspondent of a daily paper is liable no doubt to be warped by the temptation of piquancy and graphic writing; but the informants of the Government, being parties concerned, must have many inducements to suppress, colour, or garble facts which, if nakedly told, would often criminate themselves. If the tendency of the one be to exaggerate, the tendency of the others is still more clearly to extenuate and deny official failures and shortcomings; and at least the one bias is a useful and needed corrective of the other. Thus, without entering upon any disputable or irritating matters, we may refer to recent occurrences in everybody's recollection, as instances in which Ministers, even by their own admission, learned the state of affairs in the Crimea sooner, more fully, and more faithfully, through the columns of the daily journals than from their own dispatches....

But if the Daily and Weekly Press deserves its power on the score of talent, it merits it on the ground of character no less. On this head our conviction, which we do not hesitate to express strongly, runs directly counter to the common and thoughtless language of the day. In no respect does the Journalism of the Present stand out more distinguished from the Journalism of the Past – and the Newspaper Press of England from that of every other land – than in its freedom from all impure and corrupt influences. All charges to the contrary we hold to be utterly without foundation. The position and character of the men connected with all its respectable organs would of themselves be sufficient to set such sinister accusations at defiance. That it is never open to unworthy influences *of any kind*, would be too much to assert; that personal predilection or personal animosity may not often warp the judgment and blind the vision of those who wield its weapons; that individual wrongs may not occasionally lend venom to the pen of the journalist, and private hatred disguise its rancour under the fair seeming of public justice; and that party fury may not too frequently lead to a suggestion or an assertion of the false, and a suppression or a distortion of the true, – it would be absurd to deny. There may be passion, there may be faction, there may be intrigue, there may be unseemly vehemence, there may be recklessness of mischief,

there may be malice and uncharitableness, – alas! of what combatants in what arena may not these sins be safely predicted? – but from any suspicion of dishonour, corruption, or venality, the Newspaper Press of England stands wholly free. It would be as impossible to buy a journalist as to buy a member of Parliament. You might almost as well offer a bribe to a minister of state as to the editor of a leading paper.

The fact is that members of the press are open to just the same charges as members of the Legislature, and to no others. They are often as scandalously unfair. They are often as unwilling to admit virtues in an opponent or errors in a partisan. They are almost as ready to bring false imputations and almost as reluctant to retract them. They are nearly as far from the charity that thinketh no evil and that hideth a multitude of sins. Their faction about as often overrides their patriotism. They are at least as prone to fall into a tone and language which grieves the good, repels the moderate, and disgusts the courteous and refined. But those who, for the sake of what is valuable even in the most abused institutions, and in consideration of what is imperfect even in the most useful men, – bear with and forgive the disputants of St. Stephens' must acquit the controversialists of the Press.

One class of misleading influences no doubt journalists, being human, are liable to – namely, personal and social ones; and much going astray, which the unknowing public attribute to corruption, is due to these alone. These influences are natural, and not illegitimate. They only require to be watched and guarded against. It is the duty of a writer to inform and enlighten himself on the subject he is treating by every means in his power. It is his duty to keep in constant communication with those who can best supply his knowledge and correct his views. And what so informing or enlightening as intercourse with men in high place and actually engaged in the conduct of affairs? They have often materials accessible to no others; they can often by a word or a suggestion throw a flood of light upon dark matters, and place a question in its true point of view. Hence conversation with English ministers and foreign ambassadors is among the most valuable sources of wisdom and knowledge open to the journalist. And if these statesmen are skilful and courteous, it is not difficult for them to gain influence over the mind of the writer thus brought into contact with them, to place him in their point of view, to lead him to look at subjects with their eyes, to bind him to them by the tie of useful information and assistance conveyed at critical moments, perhaps even to guide or warp his judgment by the subtle operations of personal admiration and regard. An editor or writer who has thus been accustomed to go for information to a Member of the Cabinet, or who has benefited largely by the conversation of the French ambassador, or has always been kindly received at Holland House, for example, will naturally have contracted a disposition to share the sentiments and partialities of these several atmospheres; and if his other sources of enlightenment are not numerous or varied, or if his judgment be not individual and strong, he will be liable to swerve from a sound decision and a sagacious course. But the same may be said of nearly every one who lives at the great centre of affairs, – of ministers, of senators, of officials, of oppositionists: they all take the colour of the tree they feed on. The real cause for wonder is, that – considering who newspaper writers are, how well they are received by most politicians, how important it is to those in high places to

influence their opinions and supply their inspiration, and how freely many of them mingle in political society, – they should still retain so much independence and individuality of thought. We confess it has been to us a matter of perpetual surprise and no small congratulation, that the most influential and widely esteemed journals should so little reflect the tone and opinions of the best society of the metropolis – meaning by 'best,' that which is most illustrious for the rank, genius, social influence and political position of those who form it and frequent it. It is a remark-able fact, and one of great significance and consequence, that the Newspaper Press of this country, as a whole, is *not* the echo or the organ of the governing classes, – nor indeed are the more powerful and reputed journals generally the representatives or supporters of any of the several recognised parties into which the political or administrative world is divided. Wherever a newspaper is the established organ of a party, its circulation is limited and its existence precarious and costly. Journalism, therefore, is not the instrument by which the various div-isions of the ruling classes express themselves: it is rather the instrument by means of which the aggregate intelligence of the nation criticises and controls them all. It is indeed the 'Fourth Estate' of the Realm: not merely the written counterpart and voice of the speaking 'Third.' . . .

One of the most important services rendered to the nation by the periodical press consists in the exposure of abuses in various departments of the Government. These abuses are of course chiefly known to, and most thoroughly comprehended by, the *employés* themselves; and they, better than anyone, can detect them, and make their accusations good. Yet if publicity were enforced they could only do so at the hazard of their fortunes. What officer in the army or navy, or what civil servant of the Crown, could venture to denounce even the most flagrant jobs which passed under his eye, unless the custom of the anonymous sheltered him from the certain vengeance of his chiefs? Even now, as newspaper editors and popular members of Parliament well know, the difficulty is enormous of obtaining any complete or reliable information on the interior abuses in these several branches of the public service. The dread of his name being known silences many an informant who 'could else a tale unfold,' and deprives the country of much information which it ought to have. We are told that in these cases the delators need not appear in the matter themselves, but may give their information and ideas to others – to known editors and writers. But what is this but to concede the whole point at issue? since what is proposed is, not that *an* accuser, but that *the* accuser should be made responsible for all charges, – not that articles should be signed, but that they should be signed by their real authors. If all that is wanted is that *some one* shall be held answerable before the public and the law for every criticism and every denunciation, we have this already. The publisher is the legal and the editor is the virtual sponsor for everything that they suffer to appear in the columns of their journal.

It would, moreover, be found as impossible to enforce a law of publicity for the periodical press here as in France. You may compel every article to be signed, but you cannot compel it to be signed by the name of the real writer. In France the productions of the most eminent men constantly appear under obscure names.

After all, as we said at the outset, it is a question purely of comparison and degree. The withdrawal of the anonymous would render journalists more cautious, but also more timid – less

bitter and reckless, but also less resolute and daring. But whether the public would be a gainer by the change may well be doubted. And if it drove out of the ranks of political combatants – as possibly enough it might – the more polished, considerate, and modest, there can be no question that it would be to all parties a loss and not a gain.

Hitherto we have spoken of the Newspaper Press as consisting of many organs, representing every variety and *nuance* of sentiment which prevails in the community, and expressing through numerous and divergent channels that aggregate of thought, feeling, prejudice, and passion, which we term Public Opinion, – as a corporate existence, in short, comprising a thousand members whose differences and agreements, whose consenting and antagonising action, combine to constitute that power which we have described as so beneficent and vast, and that character which we have placed so high. As long as this is a true conception of the actual journalism of the country, there is little to be feared from its influence, however great that may become; the doctrines of one journal are criticised and refuted by another; the statements made in the papers of to-day are corrected or contradicted in the issue of to-morrow; and the accusations brought by the organ of one party are disproved or explained away by those of the opposing faction. The case is fully heard; the arguments *pro* and *con* are both before the court; the plaintiff and defendant are represented by pleaders whose voice reaches alike to every corner of the land. The poison and the antidote are both before us; and the antidote is disseminated as widely as the poison. In such a condition of things no injustice can easily be committed: every maligned individual is sure to find some journal who, for party or philanthropic considerations, will espouse his cause; every fallacy is certain of detection and exposure. But the case becomes widely different when from any cause one single journal has so far distanced its competitors as virtually to have extinguished them, when it has so completely monopolised the public ear, and filled the public eye, that other organs can scarcely be seen or heard. The 'republic of letters' then becomes a despotism, and menaces us with the evils which attach to autocracy in all its forms. Any decided superiority of one journal over others, once established, has an almost irresistible tendency to augment in a sort of geometrical ratio till it becomes absolute supremacy; and this supremacy, once made good, is in its nature indestructible. The leading paper is of course specially patronised by advertisers, and of course specially sought for by all those to whom advertisements are addressed: its circulation brings it advertisements; its advertisements again multiply its circulation. Again, the superior wealth which it thus acquires enables it to outbid all rivals in the command of talent; and the high reputation thus obtained makes it the favourite channel of the ablest writers. The public favour fills its coffers; and full coffers enable it to serve the public in superior style. Then, in proportion to the circulation which it possesses, is the desire of the world to read it: everybody must see what everybody else is certain to have seen. It may offend or flatter your prejudices, it may assail or support your friends, it may combat by your side or turn its weapons against you; but still you cannot do without it; you must have it; you must purchase it; and consequently you assist in maintaining the very supremacy which you deprecate. In short, its utility and superiority become such that these objects are universally sought for by the public even against their own opinion, and sometimes against their own moral

New Bridge Street

sense. Such a power then becomes something equally difficult of control or counteraction. A daily organ which has reached this paramount position, is read every morning by hundreds of thousands *who read nothing else*, who imbibe its doctrines, who accept its statements, and who repeat both to every one they meet, till the whole intellectual and moral atmosphere of the nation becomes insensibly coloured and imbued. It of itself forms, and is, the public opinion of the country. The Government knows this formidable fact, and recognises this anomalous and irresponsible power. Ministers – conscious that this omnipotent and omnipresent organ is guiding and influencing the entire active and vigorous portion of the community; that it is read by every one whose energy and enterprise affect public affairs, and that ninety-nine out of every hundred read it in a purely passive and believing spirit – dread it and consider it more perhaps than is wise or noble, but certainly not more than is natural: it becomes itself a puissance in the realm; a sole organ becomes, it is scarcely too much to say, that 'Fourth Estate' which should be the aggregate result of a multitude of conflicting and mutually modifying organs. It is as if one senator held the proxies of four hundred absentee members of the Lower House; and decided on his own responsibility the vote of an Assembly.

The 'Times,' it is notorious, has reached this extraordinary and dangerous eminence. It was not the earliest in the field; it was long before it fairly and unquestionably got the lead: but once obtained, it has never lost it. It has undeniably merited its supremacy by its vast exertions and its many excellences: it has not forfeited it by any of its lapses and offences. Sometimes it has rendered the most signal services by resolutely stemming the tide of popular phrenzy or delusion; sometimes, we think, it has done vast mischief, by echoing and encouraging the most ignorant prejudices of the people. But on all essential points – of home policy at least – it has usually been on the side of justice, freedom, and popular improvement; and, right or wrong, its ability has been always wonderful, and its unflinching courage above all praise.

We cannot here go into the circumstances which gave the 'Times' the first steps of its predominance, nor can we specify the precise moment at which it first shot ahead of its competitors. It appears to have been about the year 1835. During the last six months of that year the stamps issued to the 'Times' and 'Evening Mail' were 1,232,000, and to the 'Morning and Evening Chronicle,'* 1,004,500. Since that date the movement of the London Daily Press has been as follows: [see next page]

To a power so vast and a supremacy so unquestioned as this, we possess only three effective counteractives. Most of the other organs of the London Daily Press are, as we have seen, so far behind, that it becomes doubtful how much longer they can continue to maintain their faint and struggling existence. The last alteration of the Stamp Duty appears as if it would give them their *coup de grace;* and, as has often been the case before, a step, urged on the plea of liberty and progress, has turned to the profit of autocratic power. The provincial papers have hitherto done much to influence public opinion in their several localities and, among the non-elective classes, they are more generally read than the 'Times.' Whether the recent alteration in the law will have augmented their power as well as extended their circulation, it is too early as yet to pronounce. As the London rivals of the 'Times,' however, become one by one inoperative or extinct, the

Stamps issued to	1840	1845	1848	1850	1852	1854
Morning Chronicle	2,075,500	1,554,000	1,151,304	912,547	712,500	873,500
Morning Post	1,125,000	1,002,500	964,500	829,000	834,950	832,500
Morning Herald	1,956,000	2,018,025	1,335,000	1,139,000	1,283,000	1,158,000
Morning Advertiser	1,550,000	1,440,000	1,538,957	1,549,143	2,222,902	2,392,780
Daily News (1846)	—	3,520,500	3,053,638	1,152,000	1,228,525	1,485,100
Total†	6,706,500	9,535,025	8,043,399	5,581,690	6,281,877	6,741,880
The Times	5,060,000	8,100,000	11,021,500	11,900,000	13,225,000	15,975,740

*The 'Evening Mail' was the evening re-issue of the 'Times'. The 'Evening Chronicle' was the evening re-issue of the 'Morning Chronicle.'

†The stamps issued to these papers during the first *half* of the current year is as follows. (Parl. Paper, 438.)

Morning Chronicle	401,500
Morning Post	465.000
Morning Herald	554,000
Morning Advertiser	1,034,618
Daily News	825,000
	3,280,118
The Times	9,175,788

'Times' will inevitably more and more give its colouring and supply its materials to the organs of the Local Press, as these are more and more reduced to live upon its unchecked and uncorrected contributions. But the weekly journals – if the cheaper daily ones do not gradually drive them out of circulation – will be, as they have hitherto been, valuable competitors and correctives. They have time to consider questions more deliberately and to sift facts more carefully than those which appear from day to day; they are, some of them, conducted with considerable ability and great conscience; and one or two – the 'Illustrated News,' for example, whose leading articles are always sensible and generally very sound, – have a circulation far beyond that even of the 'Times.' That of the 'Illustrated News' now sometimes reaches, we are told, 170,000 copies. The chief and surest corrective of all, however, is, and must always be, supplied by the 'Times' itself, in the publication of the Parliamentary debates. As long as these are fully and honestly reported, no *exparte* statements of the Newspaper Press can long mislead or deceive. Every fact that concerns the public, – every charge that affects individuals, – every fallacy that has been put forth as an argument, – is pretty certain there to be sifted and exposed. And if we could

conceive it possible that any leading journal could ever make such a blunder, or commit such an iniquity as to report partially or untruly, the Houses of Parliament would have an easy and sufficient remedy in their own hands, by appointing their own reporters, and publishing their own debates. After all, however, the chief and only perfectly effective securities against the abuse of such a vast power as that wielded by a supreme journal, must be sought in the high character of those who conduct it, and in the increasing and competent judgment and instinctive sound feeling of the country, which would receive any marked dereliction from honesty or duty with disgust and indignation.

What will be the permanent effect of the abolition of the stamp on newspapers it is yet too early to predict. Probably the anticipations of those who hoped and feared great changes – certainly of those who hoped or feared sudden changes – will alike be disappointed. It was very generally believed that the removal of the compulsory penny stamp would operate an entire revolution in the newspaper press; but one party conceived that this revolution would produce vast good, the other, that it would produce vast evil. Mr. Milner Gibson and his associates fancied and hoped that journalism would be comminuted into penny newspapers, each circulating over a small district; and that the influence of the great London journals would be thus impaired and counteracted, and their provincial circulation enormously reduced. The alarmists, on the other hand, embracing most of the metropolitan, and nearly all the established local papers, while expecting a somewhat similar result, conceived that the character of the cheap journals whose competition they feared would be low and mischievous. According to the best information we have been able to collect, we are disposed to believe that there is no ground either for these excessive apprehensions or these sanguine hopes. The circulation of the 'Times' has increased since the new law came into operation; that of other metropolitan journals has, we understand (though we speak hesitatingly), somewhat fallen off. Several new cheap local newspapers have been started, but scarcely one, if one, has survived. Many of the previously existing ones, formerly weekly, or biweekly, have reduced their price, and are trying, or have tried, the experiment of a daily publication, – especially those of Manchester, Leeds, Liverpool, and Edinburgh. But the general impression left upon the minds of the more experienced proprietors and news-agents is that the *penny* papers cannot possibly succeed, and will probably be discontinued almost immediately, and that not above one or two of the cheap provincial daily papers will be able to survive when the excitement of the war and the craving for instantaneous intelligence which it creates shall be over. The reduction of price which has taken place, in some cases to 3*d*., in some cases to 2*d*. (unstamped), has of course extended the circulation of the local papers: but the habit and desire of reading a *daily* journal has to be created among the middle and lower classes, and its creation is a matter of slow growth; and the labouring poor, to whom cheapness is peculiarly important, like their paper to come when their leisure comes, viz., at the end of the week. They have a fancy for bulk too, and prefer a good deal of news at a time to a little at more frequent intervals.

That some of the more ably conducted of the daily or tri-weekly provincial journals may come into closer competition than heretofore with their metropolitan rivals, and deprive them of a

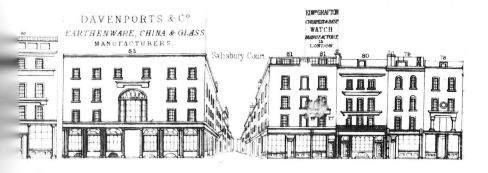

portion of their country sale, especially if the former are able to maintain their reduced price, we think highly probable. This, however, will be mainly attributable not to the removal of the stamp, but to the operation of the electric telegraph.† There is one Lancashire daily paper of great ability which contains all the latest intelligence of the 'Times' or the 'Daily News,' and is issued at half the price, and only two or three hours later than *the earliest copies* of those London journals. It receives by telegraph a summary of whatever important news those papers contain, reserving the details till the next day, and while Parliament is sitting it receives a pretty full epitome of the previous night's debate, and all this it is able to circulate throughout its own and the adjoining counties some few hours before the London journals can arrive. Thus a resident at Penrith, Lancaster, or Leeds, can receive 2 o'clock for *2d.* all the essential matter that the 'Times' would communicate to him for *4d.* at 4 o'clock; and the number of those who cannot wait till the next day for additional particulars, or for metropolitan comment, is comparatively small. How far this use, even with acknowledgment, of information which has cost the London paper large sums and which costs the local one only the price of telegraphic transmission, is strictly justifiable, we must leave to editorial consciences to determine. It is clearly beyond the reach of prevention, and we do not see that the removal of the stamp has materially, if at all, facilitated the transaction.

Walter Wellsman

This article (originally a lecture) appeared in *The Newspaper Press Directory, 1891*. The author, Walter Wellsman (1834–1911), succeeded his stepfather Charles Mitchell (founder of this pioneer work) as editor in 1859, and remained so until 1904.

FLEET STREET – 1846–1890

In approaching a subject like Fleet Street journalism, it is important to remember that of all the streets in our great City, or even in the United Kingdom, there are none more associated with the Press than Fleet Street. From almost the earliest ages Fleet Street has been the medium for communication with our great cities. It might almost be called the No. 1 Street of London, for Fleet Street was always famous as a street for news: all communications from the Government, and news and reports of all events came through Fleet Street, therefore it might very well be called not only No. 1 Street of London, but No. 1 of the world. Another reason why Fleet Street has always been the great centre of news is the fact that years ago, before the Press of England attained its present position, coffee-houses were great centres of meeting, and there the news of

the day was discussed by wits and literary men who met there. Many of such houses existed in Fleet Street, such as the Rainbow, Dick's, Peele's, and many others, and a curious history might be made of the old coffee-houses in Fleet Street; these houses in the particular style in which they were then kept have long since passed away, and clubs now occupy the places that they then filled. News letters were in many cases started from these centres, and all of us who remember Scott's novel (*Waverley*) will recollect that Colonel Talbot, in speaking to Waverley about the paper that gave an account of this father's death and his uncle's disgrace, said, "I believe there are a dozen of those confounded papers in town." The Press of England evidently took its origin in Fleet Street, or very near to it. Mr. Sala, in one of his books, says that "Fleet Street may properly be called Brain Street," and this is true, for in Fleet Street the brains of London, in the persons of the principal Press writers and contributors, may be seen daily, to say nothing of the managers of the principal London dailies and weeklies and provincial newspapers and magazines. Fleet Street in 1846 presented a very different journalistic aspect to what it now presents. There were very few newspapers published in those days; in fact, we find on reference that only thirty-five newspapers and periodicals were published in Fleet Street and the district, and only three of those papers were published daily. Now no less than eleven daily papers are published in our street and its immediate vicinity. The quality of the papers was of a very moderate character; their circulation, comparatively speaking, small; and, in fact, the only weekly newspaper said to have a large circulation in those days was the *Weekly Dispatch*, which used to boast that sixty thousand copies were sold weekly – a very moderate circulation in these days of hundreds of thousands. It is curious to notice that of the thirty-five papers then published only eighteen are now in existence, and such names as *Britannia, Gulliver, Iron Times, League, Watchman,* and *Wesleyan* are unknown even by reputation to most Fleet Street men. In 1846 the first Directory, or even list of newspapers, was published by my stepfather, the late Mr. Charles Mitchell, and it was for the first time seen in a concrete form what the Press of this country then consisted of. As a boy, and helping him with that edition, I was much interested in the Press, and that interest has never ceased from that time to this. In those days the newspapers were of a very different character to their present aspect: no telegraph intelligence, no special correspondent, few letters from abroad, but the news of the day was always, as a rule, twenty-four hours old, for the telegraph had only just then commenced its work, and the really first bit of news that I remember was telegraphed to London, and obtained currency through the medium of the Press, was a telegram from Slough to Paddington in, I think, 1845, directing the arrest of a Quaker named Tawell, who was suspected of the murder of his mistress, and by means of that telegraphic message he was arrested and afterwards became notorious as, perhaps, the only Quaker known to be executed for murder. We are used in these days to see bills stuck up at all principal newspaper offices, and to see the street flooded with small boys carrying broadsides and selling evening papers; but in those far-off days such things were rare, and I can only recollect two instances, viz., the bills that used to be put up at the *Sunday Times* office, at the corner of Fleet Street (long since cleared away for Ludgate Circus), giving the result of the principal races; and another that was stuck up in February, 1848, during the French Revolution, by the manager of a

paper then called the *London Telegraph*, published at 183, Fleet Street, stating that "the red flag floated over Paris, and that the Royal Family had fled." I well remember the crowd in the street and the interest taken in that event. Nowadays placards and bills are common, and we think nothing of them.

Perhaps one of the most interesting incidents in newspaper life in Fleet Street was the establishment of the *Daily News*, on January 21st, 1846. For a long time there had been a rumour that the newspaper was coming out on independent lines. Much had been said about this characteristic, but at last the news came that Charles Dickens was to be the editor, assisted by many well-known men, amongst them being John Forster, George Hogarth, and others. It was arranged that the paper should be published on the day after Sir Robert Peel's declaration as to the Corn Duties. The paper duly made its appearance as promised, and, though Dickens was the editor, there was nothing extraordinary about it, except the very large quantity of printer's errors, type turned upside down, &c., and to this the editor drew special attention in a letter, which appeared in the paper, directed to the master printer. Of course all this was very funny, but the paper fell very flat indeed. Dickens was not used to the drudgery of editorship, and especially the hard work entailed by a new paper, and in Forster's life we find that on February 9th, only twenty days after the paper was established, the editor resigned, and shook the editorial dust of Bouverie Street from off his feet. Arrangements were made for him to continue some connection with the paper, and he engaged to write a series of articles, which subsequently appeared, now so well known, as the charming "Pictures from Italy." This was his first and last attempt in the newspaper editing line. While speaking of Charles Dickens, it is interesting to mention that he commenced his literary life in Fleet Street. In the preface of the first cheap edition of *Pickwick*, he tells us that it was with fear and trembling he put the first contribution into a letter-box in a dark court in Fleet Street; that contribution was "Mrs. Joseph Porter," the well-known sketch in *Sketches by Boz*. The printers were in Crane Court, and it is not so very long ago, counting by years, that I found an old compositor who was present in the office when the contribution was received, and, if I am correctly informed, put it in type. The magazine was the *Monthly Review*, and was published by Messrs. McCrone and Co., of Waterloo Place. The literary history of Fleet Street, however, cannot be discussed in the short form of a lecture. It has yet to be written, but when it is, it will be of a most interesting character, not only to newspaper men, but to all literary people. I commenced some time ago to collect materials for such an enterprise, but I found such a wealth of interesting matter that I have been deterred from going on; literally from sheer excess of material, I do not see my way to spare the time yet. Let us come back to the newspapers of the time when fivepence was the ordinary charge for a daily paper, sixpence for a weekly paper, circulation but small, still the influence of the London papers was great. Everybody wanted to know what the *Times* thought, or what the *Morning Herald* said, and though in those days the growth of daily papers was very slow, they certainly increased, and gradually an interest began to be taken which soon spread. The first real step taken to popularise the daily Press of this country was in 1854, when the *Times* sent a special correspondent to the Crimea, the well-known and honoured W. H. Russell. Other papers followed their example,

amongst them the *Standard*, with its well-known writer N. H. Woods; and the daily papers, with the wonderful and interesting news from the Crimea, began at once to be looked after and read. Turning to other branches of newspaper literature, I may specially mention the religious papers. In those times they were very few, very slow, and very old-fashioned. I might even quote the opinion of a secretary of one of the then large religious associations: "That religious papers were no good; he could not advertise in them; they went nowhere, and nobody saw them." But in this branch of newspaper enterprise a marvellous change has taken place. We now see religious papers of all kinds – we may almost commence alphabetically – from the *Christian Age* to the *Christian World*. The circulation has increased to tens, even hundreds of thousands, and they are contributed to by statesmen, preachers, orators, and literary men, and are greatly thought of – I will hardly say sworn by (for perhaps religious people do not swear) – but are believed in to an enormous extent. A curious anecdote occurs to me. The editor of one of the old-fashioned religious papers, who was then editor of the *Banner and Patriot* – I allude to Dr. Campbell – was denouncing the impropriety of the ballet of those times; he said it was very shocking, highly wrong, and that young people should never see such a thing. It happened, however, that a well-known young literary man saw this article, and wrote a letter to Dr. Campbell, and asked him if he had ever seen a ballet, or been to a theatre, whether he spoke from knowledge, or whether it was mere hearsay. Dr. Campbell was obliged to admit that he had never been to a theatre. His correspondent then said he was therefore no judge on the subject, as he knew nothing whatever about it, and his opinion was worthless. So much for Dr. Campbell. The sporting papers which now abound in our streets are also a creation of the present age, or rather of the last thirty years. In the old days *Bell's Life* was the paper that all true Corinthians affected, high priced, but full of excellent sporting news; the time, however, arrived when it was thought that the sporting public could not afford the old-fashioned 6d., and a paper was started called the *Penny Bell's Life*.

However, an injunction in the Court of Chancery soon put an end to this infringement, and the title *Sporting Life* was substituted, which very soon obtained great success; but probably one of the reasons why it at once became a favourite was the great fight that took place between Sayers and Heenan. This occurred on a Tuesday, and the *Sporting Life* was published on the Wednesday, and came out with a full detail of the meeting; crowds assembled to obtain copies of the paper; police had to be employed to keep the office clear; machines worked day and night, and the *Sporting Life* then became a power in the sporting newspaper land. How the sporting papers have progressed since we all of us see; we cannot go up or down Fleet Street without being asked to purchase the *Sporting Life, Sportsman, Sporting Luck, Sporting Times,* the *Jockey,* and many others, and the penny sporting daily paper is now a necessity; when, in old times, *Bell's Life*, once a week, at 6d., was all that could be obtained. At last the old paper had to give way; its name and copyright was purchased by its great opponent, *Sporting Life*, and "Numquam Dormio," the motto of the old paper, disappeared *à tout jamais*. The ever-open eye is taking a well-earned rest. The limits of such a paper as this will not give me time to describe many of the various classes of papers that have risen up in Fleet Street, such as the illustrated papers and periodicals, the

comic papers, the trade papers, and what may be called the chatty papers, such as *Answers, Tit for Tat, Rare Bits, Tit-Bits, Great Thoughts, Pearson's*, &c. One class also I may mention is the trade organs. These are remarkable for their development, and would require a paper to themselves to do them justice. One of the greatest features in Fleet Street journalism of late years has been the influx of the provincial newspaper Press in our streets. It is not so very long ago, counting by years, that not a single provincial newspaper had an office in Fleet Street; but in the year 1868 the *Scotsman*, of Edinburgh, took a special office opposite Fetter Lane, and since then the increase has been enormous; for more than one hundred may be mentioned who have their special representative in London, scarcely one important provincial daily being unrepresented. It may be asked why is this so? It arises no doubt from the great competition, and anxiety to get business, and the increased facilities to be found in Fleet Street for obtaining news of all kinds. The question then arises, what are these facilities? Let us see. It may be remembered that somewhere in the late forties the Electric Telegraph Company was established. This was followed by the British and Foreign Telegraph Company, the United Kingdom Telegraph Company, the London District Telegraph Company, and many foreign companies also. The Electric Telegraph Company originated, if I am quite correct, the idea of supplying news to journalists, and this became a great feature, and was eagerly sought for; but after a time it was difficult for this company to keep up with every increased want, and in the year 1865 the Provincial Newspaper Society first formulated the idea of Press messages for Press people. It was difficult to carry this out, as the collection of news was practically in the hands of the old telegraph companies; but a movement took place that resulted in the Government being approached to purchase these companies (a difficult matter to commence), but in the year 1867 the Post Office authorities announced to the Provincial Newspaper Society that the Government were contemplating this step, and that the interests of the Press would be considered. It was intended, during the year 1868, to carry this into effect, but high politics raged around, and it was not until 1869 the Government, or rather the Post Office, acquired the telegraph companies, and were then in a position, for the first time, to make terms for the diffusion of news; the Press Association was constituted on a firm basis, and has since then, in conjunction with Reuter's excellent foreign Telegraphic Company, been one of the principal means of supplying provincial newspapers with telegrams of news. The association employs a large number of reporters and agents to collect and condense news, and it is then sent through the Post Office wires to their different subscribers. Such news is also supplied by another association, formed on an almost similar basis – viz., the Central News, and these two great associations keep the newspapers *au courant* with the events of the day. There is another association in Fleet Street, or very near it – viz., the National Press, who supply news in the form of stereo blocks, news in type, and in other ways to provincial papers. The effect of all this telegraphing has been to bring the news of the day almost up to the very hour of its happening, and a remarkable instance of this occurred some years ago, when the English Fleet bombarded Alexandria, when almost the number of cannon shots and shells as they were discharged were telegraphed hour by hour to Fleet Street, and appeared in successive editions of the daily and evening papers. It would perhaps astonish my audience if I told them the expenses of this. It is on record that two of our daily papers expended lately, in the one instance,

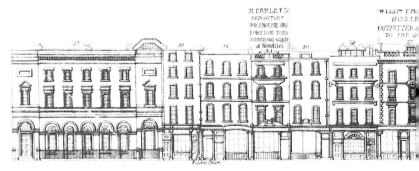

a thousand pounds in one message, and seven hundred pounds in another, and it must be remembered that these messages are scarcely copyright, for in an hour or two, at the furthest, it is copied into the other papers, and is thus made common property. It need scarcely be said with all this hunger, news is not got by the editors, sub-editors, and reporters sitting in their offices.

An illustration occurs to me: In August last, on the death of Cardinal Newman, who, it may be remembered, died on a particular Monday, the *Birmingham Daily Post* was being, as it is technically called, "put to bed" for the Tuesday morning issue, when a stranger rang urgently the office bell at half-past three a.m., and insisted upon seeing the sub-editor or someone in command. He was told the sub-editor had gone, and the boy who answered the door either left or his attention was called off, and the stranger made his way into the sub-editor's room, and seeing a rough proof of the *Birmingham Daily Post* of that morning on the sub-editor's table he put it in his pocket and walked off. To the intense surprise of the proprietors, the article written especially for the *Post* on the life of Cardinal Newman, with many interesting and original particulars, appeared in full in New York in the *New York Herald* of that morning. The stranger, in fact, was a roving correspondent, who literally annexed the copy of the paper, walked straight to the telegraph office in Birmingham, and wired it across. The proprietors, not exactly liking this way of doing business, found out the name of the gentleman, and summoned him at the police-court at Birmingham, on Monday, September 1st, on the charge of stealing the newspaper. He admitted that he had taken it, made an ample apology, and the proprietors would not pursue the matter further. I mention this to show what straits these gentlemen are put to to get early and original news. Having very briefly shown the progress of the daily Press, it will be interesting to mention that the daily Press of this country, over the whole of the United Kingdom, in the year 1846 only numbered fourteen, of which twelve were published in London, while in the present year of grace, 1890, nearly 200 daily papers are published in the United Kingdom. Perhaps some of my audience might inquire in their own minds how it is all this has been brought about. There are two reasons that will be apparent to all: first, the removal of the taxes on knowledge; second, the spread of education among the people. In 1846 the Press of this country was labouring to attain greatness under what I think I might very well call iron shackles. The Excise officers and Revenue officers dogged the steps of newspaper men and printers; there was a duty on advertisements of 1s. 6d. each, a compulsory stamp of 1d. on all newspapers, whether they wanted to post them or not, and a heavy duty on paper, so that not one pound of paper could go outside of the factory without the Revenue officer superintending its weight, and putting his stamp on each ream. Such men as Cobden, Bright, Milner, Gibson, and John Francis, the well-known manager of the *Athenæum* newspaper, persistently brought public opinion to bear on the Governments of the day. In 1853 the advertisement duty was repealed; in 1855 the compulsory stamp was removed; and in 1861, when Mr. Gladstone was Chancellor of the Exchequer, the paper duty was abolished; then the Press was at last free, and old-fashioned fogies said, "Oh yes! this is all very well, but now that everybody can do what they like without Government supervision (as they called it), we shall be flooded with atheistical and immoral publications, and the mind of our youth will be poisoned." We, however, live and learn, and I do not believe that there are more of such publications in the country at this moment than there were in those times, and as for a

Inner Temple Lane

distinctly immoral publication, he would be a clever man indeed who could find one, for I do not believe such a thing exists or can be found in the United Kingdom. Public opinion would be against it, and if it escaped prosecution it would die of inanition. I grant that there are a lot of publications published not perhaps up to the highest standard of literature, but still we must provide for the many as well as for the few. And, secondly, it is needless to say that the Education Act has done much, nay, everything, to swell the ranks of the readers, and they have been worthily catered for. The magazines and periodicals and curiosities of literature published in Fleet Street would require a lecture to themselves; they are so numerous, so various, and so important; perhaps at some future time an opportunity might be given me for a paper on them, which I am sure could be made an interesting one. With all this about the newspapers and publications in Fleet Street a word must be said about the great printers and publishers in our midst. A list of them would be but to repeat the old and well-known names of Spottiswoode and Co., Eyre and Spottiswoode (Queen's printers), Allen, Scott, and Co., Burt and Co., Bradbury, Agnew, and Co., Shaw and Sons, and many other great employers of labour, while Sampson Low and Co., and Ward, Lock, and Co., stand in the first rank among the great publishers of our metropolis. The distributors of our literature are numerous in our midst, and notably I may mention the names of Marshall and Farringdon, the household names in Fleet Street as distributors of hundreds of thousands of newspapers and periodicals. A brief recapitulation, and I have finished. In 1846 there were 35 newspapers and periodicals published in Fleet Street, three of them dailies; in 1890 there are more than 300, and 11 of them dailies. Now anyone who walks along Fleet Street, say to-day, will note that certainly on almost every other house, there are names of newspapers, engravers, publishers, and trades in connection with printing or printers. There are more or less 200 houses in Fleet Street; in 1846, 25 were occupied in such a manner, but in 1890 nearly 80 houses out of the 200 are so peopled.

It was well said "That a little nonsense now and then is relished by the wisest men," and I may, therefore, conclude by a little paraphrase of an old riddle I once heard, as to why a news boy is the happiest boy in the world. I will ask you, therefore, Why is a Fleet Street man the happiest man in London? As the answer is rather a complex one, you will perhaps permit me to give it to you. Why should a Fleet Street man be the happiest man in London? Because he has the *World* before him when he chooses, does not care a *Ha'porth* for anyone, and he can enjoy *City Life* in *Good Company* in his *Spare Moments*. He can have plenty of *Fun* with all sorts of *Funny Folks*, *Ally Sloper*, *Punch*, *Judy*, and the rest. He can have *Moonshine* when he likes, and is never without a *Star*; and there is always a *Lamp* handy in his *Office*. He need not have any anxiety about *Our Boys* and *Girls*, for they are packed off to the *Academy* by the *Housekeeper*, and taken care of by the *Schoolmaster* and *Schoolmistress*. If he is a *Sportsman* and fond of *Sporting Life* and the *Sporting World*, he can be introduced to *Paddock Life*, and see many a *Sporting Clipper*, and always have *Good Luck*. If he is a *Cyclist* and fond of *Wheeling* no *Bird of Freedom* is freer than he. If he meets with an accident he can be taken to a *Hospital*, while if a philosopher or a *Speaker* he can have *Truth* at his finger ends, while *Great Thoughts* and *Wit and Wisdom* flow from his lips.

Michael Frayn

In Tom Stoppard's play, *Night and Day*, which touches on press ethics in the twentieth century, there is the nice line: 'I'm with you on the free press. It's the newspapers I can't stand.' In this article (from *The Guardian*, Monday, 25 September 1961), journalist/dramatist Michael Frayn puts his finger on the same callused area while describing what happens when 'Lunchtime O'Booze' goes chasing moonbeams all over Europe, during the declining years, or 'anecdotage', of Fleet Street.

CEASELESSLY the British press watches over the world, informing, interpreting, explaining. Fiercely the various papers compete to devise new ways of sounding the complexities of the international situation. Well, take the "Daily Express," for example. It has just sent a man off on a quest so fantastically ingenious that it is almost impossible to describe, except in the man's own words before leaving:

"THE assignment? The capitals of Europe. Paris first. Then…? THE difference? I'll live in each capital for a few weeks, giving myself an opportunity to gauge and report the mood and spirit, to talk to the people – the ordinary and the celebrated. HOW is Paris reacting to the crisis? Is it gay, indifferent, or depressed? Are the citizens sullen, dispirited, or pleasure-bent? These are some of the questions I'll try to answer. AND these are some of the people who might help me to find some of the answers… A BEATNIK poet who believes he is the reincarnation of Napoleon. A Scots career girl who, as the French are loth to admit, has a more educated palate for wine than they have. A NIGHT-CLUB owner who imports and bottles ordinary water from Scotland as the only permissible addition to whisky."

Well, the "Daily Gasp" could scarcely ignore a challenge like that. Before closing time they had their star writer Gaylord Strewth out of the pub and in a taxi for the airport. "MY destination?" he dictated over the taxi-radio in this amazing dispatch. MY destination? EUROPE. To…? Answer the immense international question-marks. Of…? Our times.

"WHAT does sunkissed Portofino think of the Oder-Neisse question? HOW much faith do the fan-dancers of Monte Carlo have in the United Nations? THESE are some of the questions I shall be putting in the next few weeks. HERE are some of the people who will be answering them. An eccentric Swiss DOG-BREEDER with an extremely sensitive nose for fine CHEESES. A Greek FILM STARLET who believes she is the reincarnation of Marie-Antoinette. A Lallans poet who holds the Scottish All-Comers Heavyweight SPAGHETTI-EATING Championship.

By the time the third edition was running, the "Daily Gurgle" had picked the idea up, got Arthur Wynegum out of bed, and was rushing him blindly through the night.

"Off! Where to? The world's trouble-spots. Who? Me, your old pal Arthur Wynegum, for an up-to-the-minute report on the crisis. Are the passionate Slavs still eating caviar in Moscow? Is everything still ooh-la-la in gay Paree? Are the saucy Swedes as sexy as ever? These are the

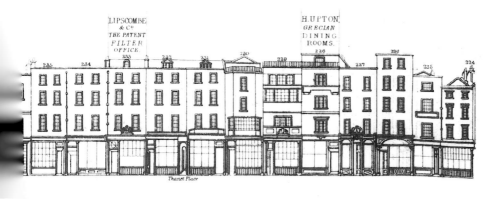

questions I shall be asking – and asking men and women who really know. A bearded lady in Athens who thinks she is a horse. The head-mistress of a swank boarding-school in Gibraltar whose hobby is collecting dustbins. An ordinary mum in Bergen-op-Zoom who walks on her hands and plays the castanets with her feet.

The "Daily Retch" just got their piece in the last edition. "At last! The FACTS about the world situation! Follow me – Cynthia Stocking, former prospective Deb of the Year, now writing exclusively in the 'Daily Retch' – around the vice-centres of Europe. Does Mr K's horoscope predict peace or war? Can prayer help? Is war most likely to break out at the full moon? Helping me to answer these searing queries on the international scene will be a pair of Siamese twins both in love with the same girl, a former cannibal chieftain now posing as a food inspector in Hamburg, and an Italian racing-driver prince who believes he is a distant relation of Rin Tin Tin."

Meanwhile, agents of a foreign power have silenced the Lallans poet by feeding him drugged spaghetti. A huge international caviar consortium is trying to bribe the Gibraltar dustbin collector to tell Wynegum that the Berlin crisis was rigged by the Ruhr smoked salmon cartel. Cynthia Stocking speeds through the night towards Hamburg in a specially hired jet airliner – little does she know that a closed Mercedes has whisked the alleged food inspector off at high speed in the direction of Magdeburg.

Is it a plot to suppress vital news? Will the British public learn the truth about the international situation? Read next week's thrilling instalment: The Bearded Lady Tells All!

Notes

1   The Place: Why Fleet Street?

1   Corrupted form of a name found in Westminster Abbey records as 'Wynandus van Woerden' – Woerden being a town south of Amsterdam, between Leiden and Utrecht. Site of the press (acc. to N. T. P. Murphy, *One Man's London* (1989) p. 150) was 32 Fleet Street and printing continued here until acquisition by John Murray in 1762.

2   David Linton and Ray Boston: *The Newspaper Press in Britain*, 1987, Introduction, p. x.

3   E. Beresford Chancellor: *Annals of Fleet Street*, 1912, pp. 51–6, 170.

4   Cited by G. A. Cranfield: *The Press and Society*, 1978, p. 11.

5   See Peter Fraser: *The Intelligence of the Secretaries of State 1660–68*, 1956, pp. 35–6.

6   Edwin & Michael Emery, *The Press and America*, 4th edn, 1978.

2   Business Forces

7   See *The Times* archives.

8   See Allen Cullen Clark: 'William Duane', *Records of the Columbia Historical Society*, 9, New York, 1906. See also Ray Boston: 'The Impact of Foreign Liars on the American Press', *Journalism Quarterly*, Winter 1973, pp. 722–30.

4   Personal Forces

9   A. J. P. Taylor: *Essays in English History*, 1976, pp. 49–54.

10   *Political Register*, I, 5, 1830, cited by Daniel Green: *Great Cobbett*, 1983, p. 187.

11   Henry Weisser: *British Working-Class Movements and Europe*, 1975, pp. 7–27.

12   William Hazlitt: *The Spirit of the Age*, 1894, pp. 285–98.

13   Louis Heren: 'All Journalists are American', *Journalism Studies Review*, I, 1976, p. 5.

14   G. A. Cranfield, op. cit., p. 115.

15   See *Black Dwarf*, 2 August 1820.

16   Joseph Nightingale: *Memoirs of the Public and Private Life of Queen Caroline*, Folio Society, 1978, p. 319.

17   R. H. Mottram: 'Town Life and London', *Early Victorian England*, ed. G. M. Young, II, 1934, pp. 175–6.

18   E. E. Kellett: 'The Press', *Early Victorian England*, ed. G. M. Young, II, 1934, p. 4.

19   A computer counting of word frequencies in 1961 singled out Sir Philip Francis as the most probable owner of this *nom de plume*. See Sybil Coady: 'Who was Junius ?', *Journalism Studies Review*, 2, 1977, pp. 39–42.

20   Alan Hankinson: *Man of Wars*, London, 1982, p. 82.

21   Asa Briggs: *The Age of Improvement, 1783–1867*, 1959, pp. 428–9.

22   W. R. Greg: 'The Newspaper Press', *Edinburgh Review*, 1855, p. 492.

23   Greg's article was commissioned in May and published in October 1855, according to Longman's Account Book, cited by *The Wellesley Index*.

24   H. Hobson, etc.: *The Pearl of Days*, 1972, p. 186.

25   Piers Brendon: *The Life and Death of the Press Barons*, 1982, p. 71.

26   F. Greenwood: 'The Press and Government', *Nineteenth Century*, July 1890, p. 110.

27   *Contemporary Review*, I, 19, p. 678.

28   G. M. Trevelyan: 'The White Peril', *Nineteenth Century*, I, 1901, p. 1047.

29   *Sell's Dictionary of the World's Press*, 1921, p. 38.

30   J. F. Gore: *The Ghosts of Fleet Street*, 1928, p. 11.

31   Harold Spender: *The Fire of Life*, London, 1926, p. 18.

32   Philip Gibbs: *The Journalist's London*, 1952, p. 3.

33   J. A. Spender: *Life, Journalism and Politics*, 1927, II, p. 167.

34   F. Lundberg: *Imperial Hearst: A Social Biography*, New York, 1936, p. 50. See also W. A. Swanberg: *Citizen Hearst*, New York, 1961, p. 117.

6   Pimps or Pimpernels?

35   Launched on the front page of the *Pall Mall Gazette* on Monday afternoon, 6 July 1885 (following an introductory leader by Stead), these sensational investigative reports and commentaries continued daily until 10 July when Part IV concluded the series.

36   In an article in the *Washington Evening Star* for 24 December 1892, an American journalist, Frank Carpenter, quotes Stead, speaking to him in his editorial office at Mowbray House, as follows: 'The fact that we have a Queen and a royal family does not affect the matter [of approaching republicanism in England]. They are of no special influence. They have their place. They are ornamental figures on our governmental tables ... But this seat here is the only true throne in England.' For the first use of this phrase, see also *Journal of W. T. Stead*,

16 April 1871, Stead Papers. The Stead Papers were deposited at Churchill College, Cambridge, in November 1986 by W. K. Stead, grandson.

37 Piers Brendon: *The Life and Death of the Press Barons*, London, 1982, p. 78.

38 Matthew Arnold: 'Up to Easter', *Nineteenth Century*, CXXIII, 1887, pp. 638–9.

39 Hugh Kingsmill: *After Puritanism: 1850–1900*, London, 1929, p. 171. In his psychoanalytical chapter on Stead, the focus is on the self-delusions of a Puritan born too late to simplify the modern world.

40 The phrase is used by A. G. Gardiner in *Review of Reviews*, October 1913, to explain why Stead seemed to him 'to challenge the judgment of his fellows in so many ways. But to all of us, whatever our opinion of his opinions, he was the prince of our craft.' The phrase was also used by John Ruskin in describing the *Pall Mall Gazette* under Stead, according to John Gross: *The Rise and Fall of the Man of Letters*, London, 1969, p. 26.

41 Ben Tillett: *Memories and Reflections*, London, 1931, p. 92.

42 Dickens shared with men such as Carlyle and Arnold an overwhelming fear of the undisciplined mob. See *Charles Dickens, A December Vision: His Social Journalism*, ed. N. Philip and V. Neuburg, London, 1986, p. 18, in which *Household Words* is described as a vehicle for what George Bagehot called Dickens's sentimental radicalism.

43 See John Morley: *Recollections*, New York, 1917, I, pp. 209–10, for Stead's self-delusions. It is also worth noting that the infamous abduction case against Stead, brought by the Attorney-General on 7 September 1885, would have failed had Stead been prepared to produce the evidence (which he possessed) that the Armstrong child was illegitimate.

44 On the confidential Cabinet information passed to Stead by Reginald Brett (Lord Esher), see Brett's letters to Stead, 29 January 1884 – 10 February 1885, in Stead Papers, and in the second Viscount Esher Papers, Churchill College, Cambridge (courtesy 3rd Viscount Esher).

45 Stead's Journal. 31 December 1882, Stead Papers. See also Frederick Whyte: *The Life of W. T. Stead*, 1925, London, I, p. 254.

46 Whyte: *Stead*, I, p. 27, cites this statement by Stead in his reported talks with John Copleston, the first editor of the *Northern Echo*, who became Stead's chief instructor in the art of editing.

47 W. T. Stead, 'Government by Journalism', *Contemporary Review*, XLIX, 1886, 667–8. He condemned 'subservient journalism' because it deprived the government of 'the advantage of friendly and independent criticism'. (Stead wrote this essay while in Holloway Gaol.)

48 A contest, run by the *Pall Mall Gazette* on 3 November 1886, for 'the worst of all newspapers', was won outright by the *Police News*, a scurrilous rag owned by George Purkess. Stead's editorial comments regarding his readers' near-unanimity makes his personal distaste of 'so many square leagues of dirtily printed falsehood' almost palpable!

49 See Estelle W. Stead: *My Father*, London, 1913, pp. 4, 21, 50. See also W. T. Stead: *James Russell Lowell: His Message and How It Helped Me*, London, 1891, pp. 9–11.

50 *Stead's Journal*, 8 August 1880, Stead Papers; Stead to Mme. Novikov, 25 August 1880, Novikov Collection, Bodleian Library, Oxford. See also Stead's claim to be 'a revivalist preacher and not a journalist by nature', as reported in *Review of the Churches*, VI, 15 August 1894, p. 298.

51 *Stead's Journal*, 23 June 1877, Stead Papers.

52 'B': 'English Journalism', *Nation*, New York, 22 July 1880, p. 59.

53 J. Hatton: *Journalistic London*, London, 1882, p. 40.

54 On the role of Edward A. Freeman, Joseph Chamberlain, W. E. Forster, and Gladstone in influencing Morley's choice of Stead as assistant editor of the *Pall Mall Gazette*, see W. R. W. Stephens: *Life and Letters of Edward A. Freeman*, London, 1895, II, pp. 35, 97, 127. Also see Gladstone Papers, BM, Add. MSS 44303, Vol. CCXVIII.

55 Whyte: *Stead*, I, p. 254. See also Arthur H. Nethercot: *The First Five Lives of Annie Besant*, London, 1961, p. 257.

56 *Contemporary Review*, XLIX, pp. 671, 673, and L, pp. 678–9.

57 'The Future of Journalism', *Contemporary Review*, L, pp. 671.

58 See Harold Evans: *Good Times, Bad Times*, London, 1983, p. 95 ff.

59 See Louis Heren: 'Declining with The Times', *Journalism Studies Review*, no. 7, 1982, p. 4.

60 See Roy Hoopes: *Ralph Ingersoll: A Biography*, New York, 1985, p. 226 ff.

61 'Future of Journalism', pp. 671, 673, 678–9.

62 Whyte: *Stead*, II, p. 33.

63 Ibid.

64 Ibid., II, Appendix II: 'Stead's Hopes for a ... unique daily paper'.

65 Ibid., I, pp. 235–42. Only Ruskin's letter was actually used by the *Pall Mall Gazette* on 8 June 1887. Shaw's letter was received and acknowledged but, surprisingly, not published.

66 Ibid. II, pp. 292–7.

67 See Max Beloff: 'Is there an Anglo-American Political Tradition?' *History*, XXXVI, 1951, pp. 73–91.

68 Brendon: *Life and Death*, p. 75. See also Whyte: *Stead*, II, p. 75. See also Stead's obituary notice for Horace Greeley, which was published in the *Northern Echo*, 5 December 1872.

69 Harold Begbie: *Albert, 4th Earl Grey: A Last Word*, London, 1925, p. 82 ff.

70 Both quotes are from Whyte: *Stead*, II, p. 238.

8 The Living Legacy

71 James Curran: 'Capitalism and Control of the Press, 1800–1975', *Mass Communication and Society*. London, 1977, p. 226.

72 Anthony Trollope: *The Warden*, London, 1946, Chapter 14.

73 Letter to the author, dated 29 February 1988.

74 Paul Ferris: *The House of Northcliffe*, 1971, p. 126.

10 Milestones and Markers

75 *The Edinburgh Review* was printed by D. Willison for Archibald Constable & Co., Edinburgh, and White & Cochrane, London.

Select Bibliography

Altick, R. D. : *The English Common Reader*, 1957

Altick, R. D.: *Evil Encounters: Two Victorian Sensations*, 1986

Archer, T.: *Highway of Letters*, 1983

Aspinall, A.: *The Press and Politics*, 1948

Aspinall, A.: 'The Social Status of Journalists at the beginning of the 19th Century', *Review of English Studies*, XXI, 1945

Barson, S., and Saint, A.: *A Farewell to Fleet Street*, 1988

Bell, Walter George: *Fleet Street in Seven Centuries*, 1912

Black, Jeremy: *The English Press in the Eighteenth Century*, 1987

Boase, Frederic: *Modern English Biography*, 1892–1921

Boyce, George (ed.): *Newspaper History: From the Seventeenth Century to the Present Day*, 1978

Brendon, Piers: *The Life and Death of the Press Barons*, 1982

Chancellor, E. B.: *Annals of Fleet Street*, 1912

Collins, A. S. : *The Profession of Letters*, 1928

Cranfield, G. A.: *The Press and Society, From Caxton to Northcliffe*. 1978

Cressey, D.: *Literacy and the Social Order*, 1980

Ellis, Aytoun: *The Penny Universities*, 1956

Escott, T. H. S.: *Masters of English Journalism*, 1911, reprinted 1970

Evans, Harold: *Good Times, Bad Times*, 1983

Foot, Michael (ed.): *The Thomas Paine Reader*, 1987

Fox Bourne, H. R.: *English Newspapers* (2 vols.), 1887

Franklin, Benjamin: *Autobiography*, 1982

Gibbs, Philip: *The Journalist's London*, 1952

Gibbs, Philip: *The Pageant of the Years*, 1946

Gore, John F.: *The Ghosts of Fleet Street*, 1928

Grant, James: *The Great Metropolis*, 1837

Greenwood, James: *The Seven Curses of London*, 1869

Hatton, J., *Journalistic London*, 1882

Hudson, Derek: *Thomas Barnes of The Times*, 1943

Kellett, E. E.: 'The Press, 1830–65', *Early Victorian England* G. M. Young (ed.), 1934

Koss, Stephen: *Fleet Street Radical*, 1973

Koss, Stephen: *The Rise and Fall of the Political Press in Britain* (2 vols.), 1983 and 1984

Lillywhite, Bryant: *London Coffeehouses*, 1963

Linton, David, and Boston, Ray: *Newspaper Press in Britain*, 1987

Mackay, Charles: *Forty Years Recollections (1830–70)* (2 vols.), 1877

Nightingale, Joseph: *Memoirs of the Public and Private Life of Queen Caroline*, 1820

Prothero, I. J.: *Artisans and Politics in Early Nineteenth Century London*, 1979

Rickman, Thomas Clio: *The Life of Thomas Paine*, 1819

Sala, G. A.: *The Life and Adventures of G. A. Sala*, 1896

Smith, A. : *The Newspaper: An International History*, 1979

Sutherland, James: *The Restoration Newspaper*, 1986

Thornbury, W.: *Old and New London* (Vol. I), 1872

Wiener, Joel: *The War of the Unstamped*, 1969

Picture Credits

The publishers thank the following for permission to reproduce their pictures. The abbreviations below indicate T: top, B: bottom, L: left and R: right.

Archive Graphics   102 (both), 122 (BR), 142 (B)

Associated Newspapers   118 (both), 119 (T), 120 (TL), 123, 127, 130 (L), 147 (T)

British Library Board   73 (TR), 86

Thomas Cook Archive   105

Ellis, Clarke & Gallannaugh   128, 129 (TL)

English Heritage   65 (LR), 73 (TL), 80, 122 (BL), 131 (TR), 145 (T), 149 (B)

Mary Evans Picture Library   38, 45, 46, 49, 52, 53, 55, 56, 61 (TL), 63 (both), 64, 65 (T), 67 (T), 75, 88, 89, 90, 98–9 (main picture), 100, 101 (T), 107, 109, 113, 116, 117 (T, BR), 120 (TR, BL, BR), 124 (BL), 125, 126 (TR), 130 (R)

Express Newspapers   153 (B)

Greater London Photo Library   47

Guildhall Library   31, 98, 155–84

Tom Hopkinson Collection   142 (T)

Hulton-Deutsch   83, 99 (TL), 104, 131 (B), 134, 136, 139 (TR, B), 143 (B), 144 (L), 145 (B), 150 (TR)

Illustrated London News Picture Library   22, 61 (LR), 96–7 (main picture), 97, 103

Caroline Irwin   40

David Kindersley's Workshop   14

London Press Club's Collection   74, 82

Mewès & Davis   93

Morning Advertiser, courtesy of the editor   92, 94

Museum of London   20

National Buildings Record   121, 122 (T)

National Film Archive   140 (T)

National Portrait Gallery   58, 69, 78, 87

Popperfoto   29, 66 (L), 119 (B), 124 (T), 126 (TL, B), 129 (TR, B), 131 (TL), 137, 138 (B), 139 (TL), 140 (B), 143 (T), 144 (R), 146 (both), 147 (B), 148 (both), 149 (T), 150 (TL), 151 (B)

Punch   10, 11, 12, 62

Royal Institute of British Architects   66–7

L. Simmonds   43

Telegraph Photographic Archive   152 (B), 153 (TR)

Times Newspapers   44, 50, 91, 124 (BL), 141, 151 (T)

Watkins Gray International   152 (T)

Index

Page references for picture captions are in *italics*. The articles 'A' and 'The' are omitted here from publication titles.